the 50 BEST STOCKS for CANADIANS

2001 edition

Philip Benson and
Gene Walden

MACMILLAN CANADA
TORONTO

First published in Canada in 2000 by
Macmillan Canada, an imprint of CDG Books Canada

Canadian Cataloguing in Publication Data

Benson, Philip
The 50 Best stocks for Canadians

Includes index.

ISBN 0-7715-7708-7

1. Stocks — Canada. 2. Investments — Canada. I. Walden, Gene. II. Title. III. Title: Fifty best stocks for Canadians.
HG5152.B46 2000 332.63'22'0971 C00-931428-8

This book is available at special discounts for bulk purchases by your group or organization for sales promotions, premiums, fundraising and seminars. For details, contact: CDG Books Canada Inc., 99 Yorkville Avenue, Suite 400, Toronto, ON M5R 3K5.

Cover & text design: Kyle Gell Design

Macmillan Canada
An imprint of CDG Books Canada Inc.
Toronto

Printed in Canada

CONTENTS

ACKNOWLEDGMENTS

This book has been a team project in the truest sense. First, I would like to thank Bill Wood for his tireless efforts in assembling this work. Bill's research and writing has traditionally covered different subject matter and I was in awe of how quickly he absorbed the jargon of P/Es, EPSs and the other sometimes arcane terms so generously tossed about by those in my profession. Bill's commitment to this project allowed me to make a similar commitment and without his dedication, the book would have never come to fruition.

I would also like to note the efforts of Andrew Winton at CDG Books. I have appreciated his tireless devotion to the project and guiding hand. I would also like to thank Robert Harris who probably could have turned to many others to work on this project but chose to give me this unique opportunity. Many thanks also to the other members of the CDG team, who compiled data, built tables and edited and proofread this book. I am sure they have never worked with someone so ignorant of publishing mechanics.

Finally, I would like to thank my family, friends and colleagues who have all encouraged me over the years in my work and who have universally lent their support for this particular endeavor.

Philip Benson

INTRODUCTION

When we were first asked about possibly writing this book, we were pulled in two very distinct directions. On the one hand, we felt that given the stock market's meteoric rise over the last several years, the timing of such a project could inadvertently coincide with a major market correction or worse. Obviously no one wants to be seen as being on the wrong side of a market turn. Weighed against these concerns were a range of beliefs we have developed about the market and investing over the last ten years that we thought could be of benefit to the individual investor, sophisticated and novice alike. We also liked the template that this project was contemplating. So with some trepidation we agreed to take on this task, though we may shy away from any public appearances if the Toronto Stock Exchange (TSE) is down 25 percent by the time this book hits the shelves!

How were we able to overcome our fears about market timing? We realized how hypocritical it was for us to have espoused to our clients over the years the notion that market timing is at best a black art and more likely a waste of time. How could it now be a good enough reason for us to worry about a book's publishing schedule?

With this in mind, here are four lessons for novice investors that we think will help readers get the most out of this book.

Lesson #1 – Don't Time the Market

There is a belief out there shared by a good number of investment pros, mutual fund administrators, and little old ladies' investment clubs that you can increase your investment success by predicting the tops and bottoms of markets. It is only possible to do this consistently in hindsight. In our opinion, the financial press does a real disservice to investors by constantly reinforcing the myths surrounding the market timing game. Every time the market drops a few percentage points, we are bombarded with headlines asking, "Is this the end?" Of course, once the market has corrected itself 48 hours later, the press and the broader investing public puts aside such potentially worrisome questions and focuses on the next quarterly earnings report or the next big deal on Bay Street. Someday the current bull market will end, and we suspect that precious few people will have accurately predicted its demise. Those that do are as likely to be tarot card readers as bank economists.

There are, of course, natural cycles to the economy, commodity prices, interest rates, exchange rates, and so on. We think that a much more useful exercise is to look at these macro-variables in the context of a specific company in which you are planning to invest or in which you currently hold a position. For example, there is a basic tenet that rising interest rates are generally negative for so-called "interest-rate-sensitive" stocks. These would include utilities, banks, and insurance companies. Obviously higher interest rates raise the cost of doing business for companies that carry significant debt levels, as is typical among utilities, or where spread business erodes, as in banks and insurance companies (for example, it is better to pay 3 percent and earn 4 percent than to pay 10 percent and earn 12 percent).

Is this to say that there are not better times to buy a given stock than to buy others? No, but usually "fine-tuning" one's investment approach requires a level of analysis that most investors cannot or will not undertake. This brings us back to our original point that, for most investors, trying to assess market timing will usually prove to be a fruitless and ultimately frustrating exercise. Far better to approach investing in stocks from the standpoint of identifying great companies that have a track record of outperformance and buying with the knowledge that someday the market may give you an opportunity to buy more of a favourite stock "on sale." Adopting this attitude towards investing will not only save you the anguish of second-guessing your buy and sell decisions, but also yield greater and more consistent investment returns.

If all of this seems a little like déjà vu, that's because what we have suggested here is classic Warren Buffet. As many readers will know, "the Seer from Nebraska" is to investing as his friend Bill Gates is to software. Buffet's style of long-term value investing is worthy of emulation. There are a good number of books available about the man and his methods, and we would encourage readers to read one if they haven't already.

Lesson #2 – Buy Track Records

We now come to the essence of this book: selecting to invest in those companies that have long established their relative outperformance. They are, in our opinion, more likely to outperform in the future. Obviously, the stock market and the various businesses and markets in which these companies operate and interact are fluid. As such, we remind the reader that what we are attempting to do with this book is to flag 50 of the best companies in Canada, not the *only* 50 companies in which you should consider investing. The 50 stocks included in this book are not necessarily all going to outperform in the future, and some may even underperform, but through diversification we are confident that a portfolio that includes a range of these stocks should deliver market-beating returns over the long term.

One of the things we have tried to do through our stock screening is to eliminate those companies whose performance could be a "flash in the pan." By applying a minimum price as of December 31, 1999, and a five-year review of our selection criteria, we feel confident that the stocks identified by our model are not the beneficiaries of short-term revenue bumps, one-time earnings gains, or inconsistent stock price and dividend growth. Again, we reiterate that no mathematical model can render a selection of companies that is guaranteed to make you money, but it can significantly increase your odds of success.

Lesson #3 – Buy Themes, Not Fads

One common investing pitfall is chasing the latest fad. The most recent example is the mania surrounding anything remotely connected with the Internet. On the other hand, a legitimate theme that has and will continue to drive the markets is the baby boom. Themes, particularly if they are long-term ones such as Canada's aging population, can help you narrow the selection of stocks you may wish to invest in by giving some sense of a given company's long-term business prospects. Fads, on the other hand, tend to be driven by hysteria and little regard for financial analysis. Sometimes a fad doesn't pass as quickly as some may predict but we would suggest that, regardless, the patient investor should not jump on the latest investment craze. By the time the average investor has read about a new "hot sector" in the newspaper, the easy money usually has already been made.

Lesson #4 – Don't Buy for the Quick Buck

It never ceases to amaze us how many people will swear that they are long-term investors who realize that stock investing is a game best played with patience. It amazes us because a good number of these people in short order suddenly remember that the $25,000 they invested six months ago was really the down payment on their new house. Once again, the bull market of the 1990s has created a dangerous condition wherein a lot of investors truly believe that the market will continue to go up with only brief periods of gut-wrenching volatility to spoil the party. While we may not experience the kinds of protracted bear markets we saw in the 1960s, 1970s, and 1980s, it is foolish to assume that they couldn't happen. We question how many people who currently have money invested in the market would be prepared to hang on to their portfolios if the market were to lose

50 percent or more of its value over a period of several years. Some readers may question such a draconian view, but history tells us that there can be extended periods of market malaise.

Besides not having a realistic view of investing time frames, there is always the tendency to buy a stock for a quick profit, often on the advice of some unidentified friend or business colleague. Every broker cringes when they get these calls from clients, for a number of reasons. First, do the "tipsters" really know what they are talking about or are they just part of a bull market rumour mill (and if they do know what they are talking about, are the broker and his or her client going to end up in jail if they act on this information!)? If a stock is in play, how much of an expected announcement's impact is already priced into the stock and what is the downside if an expected announcement doesn't happen? Is the investor really prepared to hold on to the stock if the expected quick profit fails to materialize? For the vast majority of investors, we would strongly discourage the urge to buy on impulse or with a view to making a fast dollar.

Related to all of this is a plea to do some homework. The fact that you bought this book means you probably don't need such guidance, but our experience demands that we make such mention nonetheless. Hands up if you have ever bought a stock with less thought and research than, say, a new car or TV? Enough said.

The Case for Stocks

While an individual's first investment priority should be money in the bank—everyone needs a cash cushion to fall back on—stocks should be a key component of any well-balanced portfolio. Why buy stocks rather than collecting that safe, consistent flow of interest earnings a bank account would offer? Here are some numbers to consider.

On average, over the 70 years for which records are available—which includes both the stock market crash of 1929 and the crash of

1987—stocks have provided an average annual return of about 11 percent, roughly double the return of bonds and three times the return of money market funds. The difference is even more dramatic when put in real-dollar terms. A dollar invested in bonds in 1925 would have grown to about $36 by 1999. That same dollar invested in the broad stock market would have grown to nearly $1800 during the same period. While stocks may have their ups and downs, if you can live with the volatility, you would be a far richer investor by keeping your money in the stock market.

Sometimes stock market investing requires great patience. Stock performance can vary dramatically from one ten-year period to another. An investor entering the market in 1965, for instance, would have experienced an agonizing 1.2 percent average annual return over the next ten years. But an investor in the market from 1949 to 1958 would have reaped a 20 percent average annual return. And, as you well know, the stock market in the 1990s was as profitable as in any decade of the 1900s.

Stocks or Stock Mutual Funds?

The other issue for many investors is whether to buy individual stocks or stock mutual funds. The fact is that mutual funds probably should be the investment of choice for many investors—particularly those who haven't the time, the expertise, or the resources to invest in a well-diversified selection of stocks.

But if you have an interest in the market, the time to spend researching it, and the money to diversify your portfolio, individual stocks can offer several advantages over mutual funds.

For one thing, stocks are just more fun than funds. Investing in the market can be challenging, stimulating, sometimes nerve-racking, and ultimately very fulfilling. You pit your wits against the market and against the millions of other unseen investors who are also scouring the market for a bargain. It is a test of your insight, your shrewdness.

At times, it also can be a test both of your endurance during downturns in the market and of your courage as you hold fast to your position in anticipation of that next market rally.

When you pick a winner, the results can be exhilarating. You watch the price move up. You see the stock split two for one. Suddenly your 500 shares become 1000. Your investment grows to a multiple of your initial outlay. You've won at the age-old game of picking stocks. And the victory is a boon not only to your pocketbook but also to your ego. It's that psychological reward of picking a winner that motivates so many investors to set aside mutual funds and test their hands in the stock market.

There's another important, though less publicized, reason to choose stocks over mutual funds. As they say, money is power. But it's only power if you control it yourself and decide exactly where each dollar is put to work. Socially conscious individuals who wouldn't dream of investing in companies that pollute the environment, produce tobacco products, or build weapons of mass destruction can unwittingly invest in those types of companies when they invest in stock mutual funds. Most mutual funds pay little heed to social concerns.

There are, of course, mutual funds that take a socially conscious approach and avoid investing in companies with questionable ethical connections. The problem is, when you invest in those funds you're still letting someone else decide the fate of your money. After all, you may not necessarily agree with all of the fund's ideals. You might, for instance, enjoy a beer on a hot afternoon and see no reason to avoid investing in alcoholic beverage producers. You may prefer not to invest in a company that manufactures weapons, but you may think that nuclear power is the best thing since windmills. So, a mutual fund that invests according to all of the popular ethical issues of our time may not be exactly the right investment for you. Stocks give you the freedom to make those choices for yourself.

Narrowing the List

The TSE has a universe of over 1000 stocks. How does one pick the best 50 stocks over $20 and the best 50 stocks under $20 (the subject of the companion to this book)? We selected $20 as our "bar" because, over it, one is reasonably assured of identifying larger companies. Having said that, given the bull market of the 1990s, a number of smaller companies now boast stock prices at rarefied levels. After much number crunching, many cups of coffee, and crossed eyes from staring at spreadsheets of financial data covering the last 13 years, we arrived at the following selection criteria for this book:

- Each stock is listed on the TSE
- The stock's share price must have been greater than $20 as of December 31, 1999
- Company revenues in the latest fiscal year should be at least $50 million
- Average Five-Year Return should total more than 10 percent annually
- Average Five-Year Revenue Growth should total more than 5 percent annually
- Average Five-Year Growth in Pre-tax Earnings or Earnings from Continuing Operations should total more than 5 percent annually
- The stock should not have had a negative return on invested capital in any one of the last five years

Accompanying each company profile, you will see a ratings chart similar to the one on page xv. In this chart, each star represents one ratings point. The sample company scored the maximum five points for the four categories: revenue growth, pre-tax income growth, total return, and return on capital employed. The lower left line indicates the stock's ticker symbol (in this case, ABC). The lower right line gives the total score.

Revenue Growth	★★★★★
Pre-tax Income Growth	★★★★★
Total Return	★★★★★
Return on Capital Employed	★★★★★
TSE: ABC	**20**

The following chart offers an exact breakdown of the point system for the revenue growth categories:

Growth Rate	**Points Awarded**
less than 0	-★
0 – 5%	0
5 – 7.5%	★
7.5 – 10%	★★
10 – 15%	★★★
15 – 20%	★★★★
20%+	★★★★★

Our requirement that a stock must be listed on the TSE may seem somewhat arbitrary, but the fact remains that the TSE is the senior equity exchange in Canada. Many institutional investors are precluded from buying stocks that are not listed there and the TSE is generally the most liquid of Canada's equity exchanges.

The $20 share price may strike some as even more arbitrary than the TSE listing requirement, but we chose this cut-off to group stocks into smaller and larger market capitalization. Given the bull market of the 1990s, a lot of smaller companies boast stock prices well in excess of $20, so we caution the reader that this criterion cannot be relied upon to sort blue-chip stocks from speculative stocks.

By mandating that a company have at least $50 million in consolidated revenues, we have attempted to address the risk identified in using a $20 stock price as our cut-off. By mandating revenues in excess of $50 million, although we may not have eliminated smaller companies from the selection process, at least there will be no "start-ups."

The next four criteria were selected to identify those companies that have generated above-average financial performance over the last five years. By using a five-year window, we hope to eliminate those "flash-in-the-pan" results that some companies are able to generate. Note that a negative result for any of the five-year totals results in a loss of one point.

We should make a comment about "five-year total return" and "positive returns on invested capital," as these concepts may not be familiar to the reader. With five-year total return, we are looking at a combination of the company's stock price appreciation (or depreciation!) added to the yield provided by any common share dividends paid. Because of the popularity of share repurchase programs in lieu of dividend payments or increasing dividend payments, this allows us to look at companies on an "apples-to-apples" basis.

We have mandated a positive return on invested capital as, again, this is a decent measure of management's effectiveness in generating a return for each dollar of the shareholder's and debtholder's money. More commonly, investors focus on return on equity, as this singles out the "stock component," but we feel that a broader measurement of corporate performance is preferable. In other words, this criterion discounts those companies that may be able to generate high levels of return on equity by carrying overly burdensome debt levels.

In situations where there were tie scores, we used trailing twelve month price to book value per share measurements to determine the order in which the stocks would rank. Book value per share is considered by many to represent the networth per share of a company, and by comparing this to the price, we can determine the best values among similarly ranked stocks.

The selection of these particular criteria has resulted in the exclusion of some companies that will probably surprise a lot of investors. For example, why isn't Nortel Networks on this list? The answer lies in its rather dismal earnings performance in 1998 that, at the time we screened our database, excluded it from the final selection even though it had impressive numbers across the other criteria. It is quite possible that Nortel's 1998 results will prove to be an aberration, but we are hesitant to second-guess a selection process that is meant to identify not just good financial performance but consistency as well. And investors would have done almost as well over this period by owning stock in Nortel's parent company, BCE, with arguably less risk and volatility.

Performance Graphs

At the end of each profile, you will see a five-year financial *At a Glance* summary of the company's performance, including revenue, net income, earnings per share, dividends per share, dividend yield, and price-earnings (PE) ratio. Unless otherwise indicated, all revenue and income amounts are in Canadian dollars.

Also included is a "high-low-close" stock growth chart similar to the one shown below.

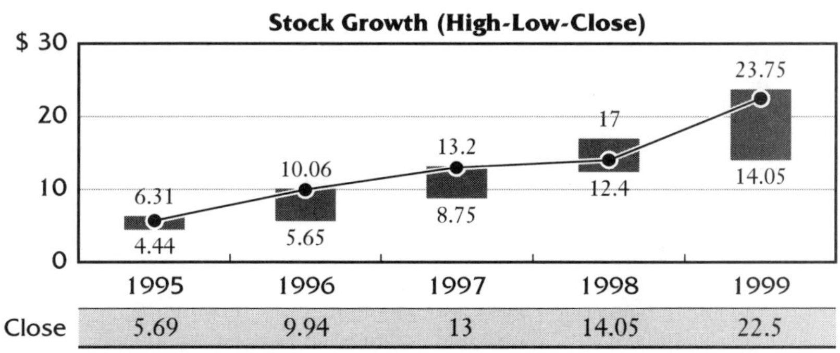

This stock graph shows the yearly stock price range (all figures are adjusted for stock splits), including high price for the year, low price for the year, and closing price for the year.

Now you're ready to begin making this book work profitably for you!

HOW TO USE THIS BOOK PROFITABLY

Think of this book as a sales catalogue for investment shoppers. You can page through it, look over the merchandise, and make your selections.

Let's assume that you have $20,000 to invest in stocks. Here is the process we recommend that you use to select the best stocks for you based on the entries in this book:

1. Begin by reading through the 50 profiles and narrowing your choices to 10 to 12 stocks by asking the following questions:
   - Are they companies you like?
   - Are they involved in business activities that you think have a strong future?
   - Are they located in your part of the country? This is not essential, but it is easier to follow companies based close to your home because the local press tends to give those companies better coverage and you can stay better informed on your investment.
   - Do they represent a diverse cross-section of industries? Spread your choices around. You might select a financial institution, a computer manufacturer, a medical products firm, a retailer, a food company, a consumer products manufacturer, and a telecommunications operation. Choose no more than two or three companies from the same industrial segment. By selecting a broad portfolio, you can minimize your losses if one sector goes sour.

2. The next step is to narrow your list of 10 to 12 favourites to the 4 to 6 companies that you will ultimately invest in.
3. If you wish to use a stockbroker or financial adviser, call your adviser, read him or her your list of choices, and ask if he or she has any current research on those stocks. If so, find out which ones your broker recommends and buy the stocks through your broker.

Going It Alone

If you do not have a broker or wish to go it alone through a discount broker, here are some steps you can use to narrow your list to the four to six companies you will ultimately invest in:

1. Write to or call the 10 to 12 companies you are considering to request their annual reports and their annual information forms (which are supplements to the annual reports), then skim through the reports. (The phone numbers and addresses of each of the 50 companies in this book are listed along with their corporate profiles.) You can also go online and visit their Web sites. We have listed Web sites for companies where possible.
2. Look up recent articles on the companies on the Web or at the library. If it's a local company, there's a good chance your library will have an entire file on the firm. Make sure that the company hasn't become involved in any major scandals or business problems. The library also may have two or three investment research books you can use to check up on your potential stock selections.
3. Keep an eye on the stock prices of the companies in which you are interested. Find out at what range each stock has been trading over the past few months. Then select the four or five stocks that appear at present to be the best values.

Timing can be very important to your overall success. All stocks fluctuate greatly in price, tugged along by the current of the overall market. Some stocks vacillate more than others do. Even for stocks that qualify as a 50 Best entry, timing can make a significant difference.

When to Buy

Volumes have been written on this topic. But the best advice may have come from Baron von Rothschild in the mid-1800s. He said, "Buy when the enemy is at the gate and sell when you hear your cavalry's bugle sounding charge."

Bay Street has a popular adage that reinforces this concept: "Pessimism is always most rampant just before the market hits bottom."

Two extraordinary buying opportunities have arisen in the past several years. The first came in 1987 following the October "Black Monday" crash. The crash frightened many investors out of the market, but those who bought when everyone else was selling got in on the bottom of a market that grew more than 50 percent over the next 18 months.

The second great opportunity came during Iraq's occupation of Kuwait, when oil prices were rising and the world was transfixed by the Middle East crisis. The market dropped about 15 percent in the months after Iraq invaded Kuwait, then roared back more than 20 percent in a three-month span that began on the day that the Allies started bombing.

Barring war or disaster, the best strategy for most investors is a steady, persistent, long-term investment program.

Though investors may strive to buy stocks while they are well below their peak prices, market experts advise against buying a stock on its way down. Or, as they say in the brokerage business, "Don't fight the tape." Wait until a falling stock has bottomed out and shown some upward momentum before buying.

Benefits of Dollar Cost Averaging

One of the easiest and most effective investment strategies is called dollar cost averaging, and it's as simple as this: Pick a number, any number—$100, for instance—and invest that amount every month (or every quarter or every year) in the same stock. Period. It's that simple. Elementary as it sounds, however, the dollar cost averaging method is also a very effective technique for beating the market. Why? By sticking to a set sum each time you invest, you automatically buy fewer shares when the stock price is high and more shares when the price is low.

The following table illustrates the advantages of dollar cost averaging. The table assumes that the stock price fluctuates somewhat each month (and lists the monthly price of the stock). The table compares the number of shares purchased through a dollar cost averaging method with the number of shares purchased through a method in which the investor buys a set number of shares each month.

Example of Dollar Cost Averaging
(Investing a set dollar amount each month versus buying a set number of shares each month.)

Month:	Jan	Feb	Mar	Apr	May	June	July	Aug	Sept	Oct	Nov	Dec	Totals
Stock Price[1]	$10	9	12	13	9	10	8	7	9	12	10	11	
Investor A Dollar Cost Averaging[2] Investment:	$100	100	100	100	100	100	100	100	100	100	100	100	$1200
Shares	10	11.1	8.3	7.7	11.1	10	12.5	14.3	11.1	8.3	10	9.1	123.5
Investor B Set Quantity[3] Investment:	$100	90	120	130	90	100	80	70	90	120	100	110	$1200
Shares	10	10	10	10	10	10	10	10	10	10	10	10	120

1. Indicates average stock price each month.
2. Assumes investor invests $100 per month in the stock.
3. Assumes investor buys 10 shares of the stock per month.

As the table indicates, by using the dollar cost averaging method investor A would have purchased 3.5 more shares than investor B, who bought a set amount of shares each month, even though both spent a total of $1200 during the year.

Tip: The dollar cost averaging method is most effective when you make your purchases at no commission (or at minimal commission) through a company's dividend reinvestment and voluntary stock purchase plan. Such plans are ideal for dollar cost averaging because they enable you to buy fractional shares and to make regular contributions (some companies offer stock purchase options once per month, others once per quarter). However, if the company you're interested in has no stock purchase plan, the brokerage commission you would have to pay to make regular investments in the company's stock would greatly diminish the advantages of a dollar cost averaging plan. Contact the investment relations offices of the companies you are interested in to find out which companies offer a dividend reinvestment and voluntary stock purchase plan.

Picking Winners

There is no infallible system for predicting tomorrow's market winners—only ratios and theories and computer-generated formulas that seem foolproof but aren't. For investors who trade actively in stocks, the key to beating the market is not so much which stocks to buy, but when to buy them and when to sell them. And that's about as easy to predict as next month's weather.

Even Bay Street's finest can't consistently outfox the market. Stock mutual funds offer an interesting example. Despite being actively managed by some of the sharpest, most well-supported analysts in the investment industry, the average rate of return of stock mutual funds traditionally trails the overall market averages. Generally speaking, history has shown that you can do better by simply buying and holding a representative sample of stocks—without ever making a single trade—than most mutual fund managers do with their wealth of investment research, their finely honed trading strategies, and all of their carefully calculated market manoeuvres.

For sustained, long-term growth, it's hard to beat a buy-and-hold strategy. Buy good companies with the intention of holding on to them for many years. But if the companies show little progress during a period when most of the rest of the market is moving up, it may be time to look for more promising stocks.

The Strategy of Benign Neglect

Most of us know someone who bought a few shares of a stock many years ago, stashed the certificates in a drawer, and then discovered years later that the stock had grown to a multiple of the original cost. Benign neglect is often the smartest policy for stock market investors. Besides avoiding the difficulties of making timely buying and selling decisions, the buy-and-hold approach offers some other excellent advantages.

No commission costs. Let's assume that you turn over your stock portfolio just once a year. You sell all of the stocks you own and buy new stocks that you think have greater short-term potential. Typically, you would incur about a 2 percent commission to sell the old stocks and a 2 percent commission to buy new ones—a total of 4 percent in round-trip commissions. That means, for instance, that a respectable 12 percent gain on your investments would suddenly shrink to 8 percent after paying off your broker. That commission may not seem like much at the time, but over the long term it can add up to a significant amount. See the chart on page xxv on the hidden costs of a buy-and-sell approach. (Online brokers have cut those costs considerably. Most online brokers offer trades for approximately $29, regardless of how many shares you buy or sell.)

Tax-sheltered savings. A buy-and-hold strategy is one of the best tax-advantaged investments available today. You pay no taxes on the price appreciation of your stocks until you sell them—no matter how long you keep them. (However, you are taxed on any stock dividend income.) Every time you sell a stock, the federal government taxes you on your gains. Provincial taxes are also applied to capital gains. That means that each year you would lose a substantial portion of your investment profits when you sell your stocks. How does that translate into real dollars?

Let's assume that you start with an investment of $10,000; your stock portfolio appreciates at a rate of 12 percent per year; and you sell your stocks, take the profit, and buy new stocks once a year. The following chart compares your performance with that of a buy-and-hold investor with an identical 12 percent compounded average annual appreciation rate.

The Hidden Costs of a Buy-and-Sell Approach

	Buy-and-hold	**Buy and Sell Results (1)**	
$10,000 investment @ 12% annual growth	(No commission)	With commission(2)	And with taxes(3)
After 1 year	$ 11,200	$ 10,800	$ 10,500
After 5 years	17,600	14,700	12,760
After 10 years	31,000	21,600	16,290
After 20 years	96,500	46,600	26,530
Total 20 year profit (minus initial $10,000)	$ 86,500	$ 36,600	$ 16,530

Notes:
1. Assumes investor sells all stocks in portfolio one time per year (and reinvests in new stocks).
2. Assumes commission of 2% to buy and 2% to sell (an annual total of 4% of total portfolio price).
3. Assumes a combined capital gains tax rate of 50% on 75% of all profits.

As you can see, over a 20-year period the buy-and-hold portfolio could earn over five times the profit of a buy-and-sell approach—even though both portfolios earn an average annual return of 12 percent.

Less emotional wear and tear. By adhering to a buy-and-hold strategy, you also avoid the high anxiety of trying to buy and sell stocks actively—watching the financial pages each day to see how your stocks have fared and enduring the inevitable disappointment of watching them rise and fall, then rise and fall again. Every stock goes through many ups and downs each year. There are no exceptions. The market moves like the tide of the ocean, and every time it ebbs and flows it carries with it the broad market of individual stocks. Typically, about 70 percent of a stock's movement is attributable to the stock market itself. If the broad market is moving up, almost any stock you pick will also rise. If the market is in a tailspin, almost any stock you pick—even those with record earnings—will fall with it. The remaining 30 percent of the movement of a stock is attributable to its industry group and to the performance of the company that issued the stock.

You avoid much of the emotional pressure that the market inflicts if you invest with a buy-and-hold approach. You don't have to concern yourself with the inevitable daily ups and downs—or even the yearly ups and downs—of the market. Over the long term, if you've bought stocks of good, solid, growing companies, the value of your portfolio will eventually reflect the strong performance of those companies. That's why it's crucial to select your stocks carefully—that one decision takes on much greater importance.

When Not to Buy

Assuming that you've selected 10 to 12 prospective stocks, that you've researched the companies, and that you're ready to buy, what financial factors should you look at to decide which 4 to 6 of those prospective stocks represent the best value at the time?

The easiest way to select your finalists might be through a process of elimination: Weed out the stocks that appear to be overvalued and invest in the others.

To assist you with your elimination process, here are two of the most common "don'ts."

Don't buy when a stock is at an all-time high. Stocks constantly rise and fall. A noteworthy adage in the securities industry goes like this: "The market always gives you a second chance." In almost every case, when a stock reaches an all-time high, it will eventually drop in price, bounce back up, and then drop again. Nothing goes in a straight line. If you see that a stock is at its all-time high, it's probably not a very good value at that time. Prior to the October 1987 crash, many stocks were at or near their all-time highs, which is one reason why many investment experts claimed—correctly—that there were few good values in the market.

Don't buy when the price-earnings (PE) ratio is unusually high. It sounds complicated, but the PE ratio is actually a very simple formula that offers yet another barometer of a stock's relative value. And best of all, the PE ratio is listed along with the company's stock price in the financial section of most newspapers, so you don't have to calculate it yourself. Specifically, the PE ratio is the current price of the stock divided by the company's earnings per share.

Example:
ABC Corporation's stock price is $30.
Its earnings per share are $3.
Stock price ÷ Earnings per share = PE ratio
$30 ÷ $3 = 10

PE ratios are like golf scores—the lower the better. Generally, the PE ratios of most established companies are in the range of 10 to 20 (although a handful of the stocks listed in this book have higher PE ratios and a few have PE ratios under 10). The real key is not how the PE ratio of one company compares to that of another, but how a company's current PE ratio compares to its own previous PE ratios.

In this book, at the end of each company profile you will see a financial *At a Glance* table that shows the company's PE ratio for the past five years. You might use that PE ratio as a guidepost to provide a relative point of comparison.

If you find on comparing the company's current PE ratio (as listed in your morning newspaper) with its past PE ratio range (as listed in this book) that the PE ratio is near or above the high end of its past range, that could be an indication that the stock is relatively overvalued.

When to Sell

The decision of when to sell is best made before you ever buy. Decide then how low you're willing to go before you sell, how long you'll wait for the stock to move, and how high you hope to ride the stock before you sell it.

The most common mistake that investors make in selling their stocks is to sell their winners to take a (fully taxable) profit and hold on to their losers in hopes that those stocks will someday rebound. That's an excellent way to assemble a portfolio of losers. Prevailing wisdom in the investment business calls for just the opposite approach: "Cut your losses and let your profits run."

With that in mind, you might consider following a couple of basic strategies for selling stocks.

Sell when the news is grim. If you own stock in a company that comes under legal siege or becomes involved in some type of disaster or health controversy, take your lumps and get out as fast as you can dial up your broker.

Sell when the stock price drops relative to the market. Barring disaster, you also might want to set up another type of safety valve for your stocks. For instance, if the stock drops 10 to 20 percent while the market in general is moving up, it might be time to move on to something more promising. Some investors use a 10 percent/10 percent rule in which they sell a stock when it drops 10 percent from its recent high and drops 10 percent relative to the market. For example, if your stock drops 10 percent from $100 to $90, it meets the first criterion. But if the market in general has also gone down with your stock, then the stock hasn't met the second criterion. If, on the other hand, the broad market has stayed the same or moved up while your stock has dropped 10 percent, then it's time to sell—based on the 10 percent/10 percent rule.

Patient investors might lean towards a modified version of this rule: the 20 percent/20 percent rule. If your stock drops 20 percent and drops 20 percent relative to the market, sell it and move on to something more promising.

Sell when earnings drop. Investment professionals sometimes call it the "cockroach theory." When you see one disappointing earnings report, that may mean that more bad periods are looming around the corner—just as the sight of a single cockroach usually means that others are hiding under the sink or behind the cupboard. Money managers who follow the cockroach theory get out of a stock at the first sign of trouble—even if it means taking a small loss now to avoid taking a bigger loss later should the bad news continue.

Sell when the company no longer meets your investment objectives. If you bought a stock because the company had enjoyed 40 consecutive years of record earnings, you should continue to hold the stock as long as the company continues to pile up record earnings. But if it hits a slump and its earnings stop growing, that company no longer meets your objectives. That's a good time to sell. Weeding your portfolio every two or three years can help make you a more successful investor.

Timing can be a tricky business. Sometimes you will be better off holding on to a stock rather than selling it. That's why your buying decision is so important. This book can help steer you to 50 of the best stocks in Canada.

A Final Word

Clearly the market provides opportunities to make profits in very short periods of time. Modern technology has increased the speed with which information is disseminated and ultimately reacted to in the capital markets. We would argue that there are two types of people who buy stocks: investors and traders. Investors are primarily concerned with information as it pertains to specific industries and companies and look at stock prices almost as a secondary activity. They generally have a long-term investment horizon and pay little or no attention to day-to-day fluctuations in the markets. They read research reports and annual reports and research the fundamentals of trends and themes to help them arrive at investment decisions.

Traders, on the other hand, are primarily concerned with stock prices and their direction and concern themselves secondly with company-specific information. They are more interested in the volume at which a stock is trading and its relative strength, not in what the CEO of the company enunciated as his or her five-year plan. Whether they plan to hold a stock for 24 hours or 24 days, few traders can envision holding it for anything other than the short term.

Both investors and traders can make money in the stock markets, but with history as our guide, we are convinced that investors have the edge. This book is for investors.

1

DOREL INDUSTRIES INC.

1255 Greene Avenue, Suite 300
Westmount, PQ H3Z 2A4
(514) 323-5701
www.dorel.com

President, Chairman, CEO: Martin Schwartz

Revenue Growth	★★★★★
Pre-tax Income Growth	★★★★★
Total Return	★★★★★
Return on Capital Employed	★★★★★
TSE: DII.B	**20**

Dorel Industries is a furniture and consumer products manufacturer. Its business is divided into three segments: ready-to-assemble (RTA) furniture, juvenile (infants'/children's) furniture and accessories, and household furnishings.

Dorel's RTA segment (the fourth-largest RTA producer in North America, according to the company) includes home-office furniture, kitchen and storage units, and entertainment units. The juvenile segment (the third-largest in the United States, with such brand names as Cosco) produces cribs and beds, high chairs, and strollers and car seats (including a line of Eddie Bauer brand products). The household furnishings segment produces metal bunk beds, futons, home-office furniture, and stepstools and folding tables and chairs.

For fiscal 1998 Dorel's RTA segment represented 39 percent of sales of $767 million, while the juvenile segment accounted for 38 percent and household furnishings represented 23 percent.

For the nine-month period ending September 30, 1999, Dorel reported revenues of $680 million, a roughly 25 percent increase over the same period in the previous year.

The company made two significant acquisitions during fiscal 1998: Ameriwood, a U.S. RTA manufacturer, for US$41 million; and Arkansas-based wooden crib and dresser manufacturer Okla Homer Smith for US$7.25 million (Dorel is already North America's leading metal crib manufacturer).

Headquartered in Montreal, Dorel employs over 3300 people in 9 countries (the majority of employees are in North America). Its products are sold in over 60 countries, although the vast majority of sales are in the United States: 87 percent in fiscal 1998, with 51 percent going to Wal-Mart and Kmart alone. Canada accounted for 4 percent of sales in the same period.

Clearly Dorel has benefited from baby boomers' desire to "do it themselves"; as those in this segment of the population enter their retirement years, there is no reason to expect they will want to do any less. As homes are sold in favour of vacation properties and smaller condominiums and townhouses, there should be good demand for new furnishings.

Dorel is listed on the Toronto, Montreal, and NASDAQ stock exchanges.

Revenue Growth: ★★★★★
Past five years: 25 percent

Pre-tax Income Growth: ★★★★★
Past five years: 53 percent

Total Return: ★★★★★
Past five years: 47 percent

Return on Capital Employed: ★★★★★
Past five years: 21 percent

Dorel Industries Inc. at a Glance

Fiscal year ended: December 1999

Revenue and net income in $ millions

	1995	1996	1997	1998	1999	4-Year Growth Average (%)	4-Year Growth Total (%)
Total Revenue	388	426	532	767	929	25.01	139.58
Net Income	11	16	25	27	56	55	416.52
Earnings/ Share ($)	0.44	0.62	1	0.97	1.91	49.03	334.09
Dividend/ Share ($)	0	0	0	0	0	–	–
Dividend Yield (%)	0	0	0	0	0	–	–
Price to Earnings (PE)	10.8	15.32	17.5	25.57	13.53	–	–

Stock Growth (High-Low-Close)

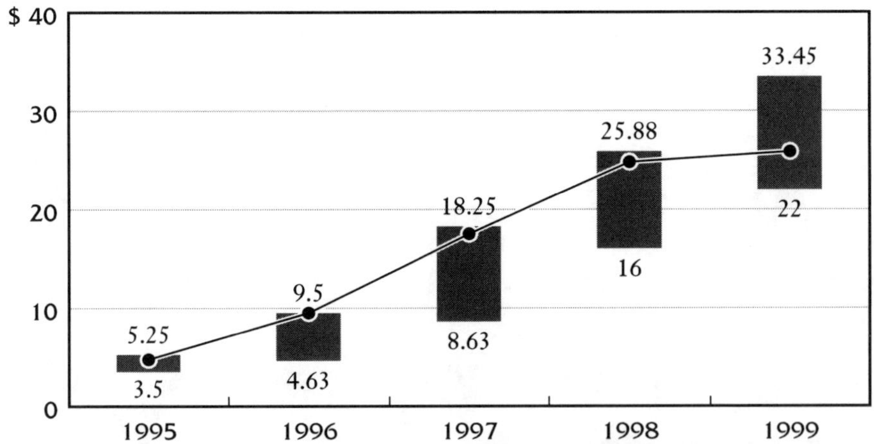

Close	4.75	9.5	17.5	24.8	25.85

2

ATI TECHNOLOGIES INC.

33 Commerce Valley Drive East,
Thornhill, ON L3T 7N6
(905) 882-2600
www.ait.com

President, CEO: K.Y. Ho

Revenue Growth	★★★★★
Pre-tax Income Growth	★★★★★
Total Return	★★★★★
Return on Capital Employed	★★★★★
TSE: ATY	**20**

ATI Technologies Inc. designs, manufactures, and markets 3-D graphics and multimedia technology, particularly components such as graphics accelerator chips. These products are sold to both consumers and manufacturers (for integration into such products as computer motherboards and television "set-top" boxes).

The investment focus in the personal computing market has usually been on the major hardware manufacturers (e.g., Dell) or the software vendors (e.g., Microsoft). Companies like ATI Technologies represent another way to invest in this fast-growing sector. In fact, as the bandwidth of the Internet expands to allow faster downloading of complex graphic and video files, the graphics capability of PCs will increase significantly. This obviously bodes well for this company.

Sales for fiscal 1999 (year ended August 31, 1999) amounted to US$1.2 billion, versus US$737 million in fiscal 1998. For the first half of fiscal 2000 (ending February 29, 2000), the company reported sales of US$794 million.

In fiscal 1999, the company's sales were divided geographically as follows: 36 percent in the United States, 34 percent in Europe, 26 percent in Asia, and 4 percent in Canada.

This is unquestionably a fiercely competitive market and companies such as ATI struggle to maintain their leadership positions. In fiscal 1999, ATI spent US$122 million (net) on research and development (approximately 10 percent of sales). ATI estimates that products in its marketplace have a lifecycle of 12 to 18 months due to the rapid pace of technological advancement.

As of the end of the second quarter of 2000, ATI was the world's leading provider of 2-D, 3-D, and video integrated graphics chips for the mobile computing market, as well as the leading provider of 2-D/3-D and video graphics accelerators to original equipment manufacturers (OEMs) and retail customers.

ATI is headquartered in Thornhill, Ontario, with additional offices and facilities in the United States, Germany, France, the UK, Ireland, Barbados, Malaysia, Japan, and Hong Kong. The company employs approximately 1,800 people worldwide.

Shares of ATI are traded on the Toronto and NASDAQ stock exchanges.

Revenue Growth: ★★★★★

Past five years: 60 percent

Pre-tax Income Growth: ★★★★★

Past five years: 107 percent

Total Return: ★★★★★

Past five years: 42 percent

Return on Capital Employed: ★★★★★

Past five years: 30 percent

ATI Technologies Inc. at a Glance

Fiscal year ended: August 1999

Revenue and net income in US$ millions

	1995	1996	1997	1998	1999	4-Year Growth Average (%)	4-Year Growth Total (%)
Total Revenue	308	407	533	1,156	1,838	59.73	496.53
Net Income	14	24	42	168	160	111.64	1,077.42
Earnings/ Share ($)	0.067	0.123	0.208	0.784	0.731	105.71	991.04
Dividend/ Share ($)	0	0	0	0	0	–	–
Dividend Yield (%)	0	0	0	0	0	–	–
Price to Earnings (PE)	33.58	22.36	28.03	21.24	24.21	–	–

Stock Growth (High-Low-Close)

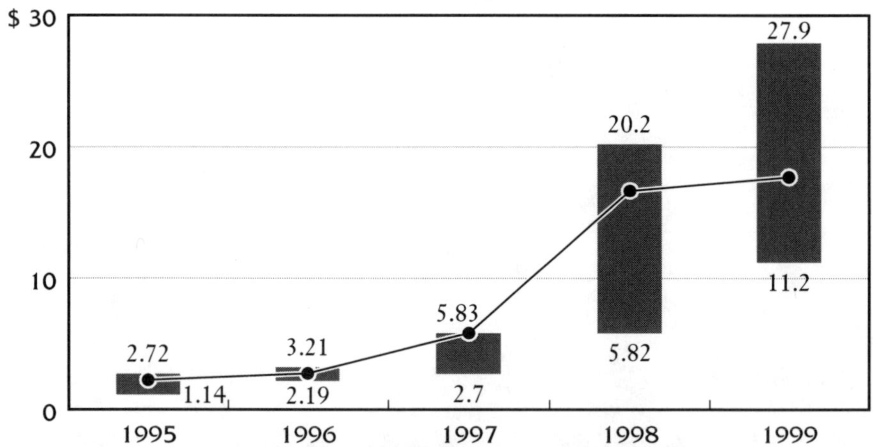

Close	2.25	2.75	5.83	16.65	17.7

3

CREO PRODUCTS INC.

3700 Gilmore Way
Burnaby, BC V5G 4M1
(604) 451-2700
www.creo.com

CEO: Amos Michelson
President: Daniel Gelbart

Revenue Growth	★★★★★
Pre-tax Income Growth	★★★★★
Total Return	★★★★★
Return on Capital Employed	★★★★★
TSE: CRE	**20**

The printing press has been one of the most basic pieces of machinery to have transcended the cycle of technology obsolescence so common in other industries. While they have become bigger and faster over time, the basic "technology" of a printing press has changed little in the last hundred years. However, that is now changing; we are at the dawn of a new age in the creation of the printed word. Creo Products Inc. develops, manufactures, markets, and services digital prepress equipment for the commercial printing industry (the prepress phase of the printing process involves the creation of master printing plates).

The company has experienced phenomenal growth over the last few years, with revenue expanding at a better than 40 percent annual clip and a corresponding income jump averaging 100 percent. Revenue for fiscal 1999 (year ending September 30, 1999) was US$178 million, versus US$129 million for fiscal 1998. For the first six months of fiscal 2000 (ending March 31, 2000), the company reported revenue of US$117 million, versus US$78 million for the same period a year earlier.

Geographically, the company's fiscal 1999 revenue was divided as follows (all figures in US dollars): United States, $106 million; Europe, $56 million; Canada, $4 million; Japan, $3 million; other, $9 million.

The company has operating subsidiaries in the United States and Belgium to support its U.S. and European business. The company's "computer-to-plate" systems have been installed in 32 countries, and nine of the ten largest North American commercial, catalogue, and publication printers use the Creo's products. While the "digitization" of our broadcast and telecommunication infrastructure is widely publicized, its penetration of traditional print media is not as well understood. Creo estimates that less than 20 percent of the world's printers use a "computer-to-plate" system, suggesting that there are growth opportunities awaiting the company.

In 1997, the company began a joint venture with Heidelberger Druckmaschinen AG, the world's largest printing press manufacturer, to develop, manufacture, and market select prepress equipment and related materials. Joint venture business accounted for approximately 32 percent of fiscal 1999 revenue.

The company is headquartered in Burnaby, British Columbia, and, as of September 1999, employed approximately 1,500 people worldwide.

Revenue Growth: ★★★★★

Past five years: 41 percent

Pre-tax Income Growth: ★★★★★

Past five years: 101 percent

Total Return: ★★★★★

Past five years: 625* percent

Return on Capital Employed: ★★★★★

Past five years: 31 percent

* Note: Total Return figure is based on growth in common share equity since 1995. Creo only went public in July 1999.

Creo Products Inc. at a Glance

Fiscal year ended: September 1999
Revenue and net income in US$ millions

						2-Year Growth	
	1995	1996	1997	1998	1999	Average (%)	Total (%)
Total Revenue	–	–	132	197	262	41.04	98.22
Net Income	–	–	8	17	27	85.52	237.86
Earnings/ Share ($)	–	–	0.331	0.628	0.866	63.81	161.63
Dividend/ Share ($)	–	–	0	0	0	–	–
Dividend Yield (%)	–	–	0	0	0	–	–
Price to Earnings (PE)	–	–	–	–	43.3	–	–

Stock Growth (High-Low-Close)

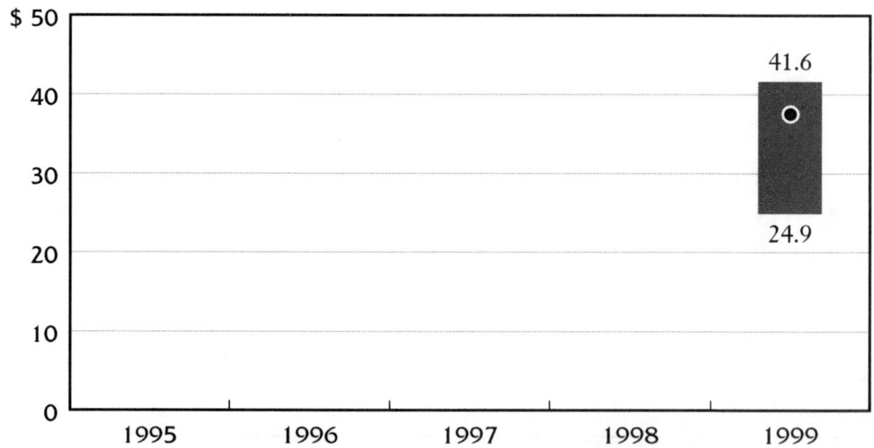

Close	1995	1996	1997	1998	1999
					37.5

4

CGI GROUP INC.

1130 Sherbrooke West, 5th Floor
Montreal, PQ H3A 2M8
(514) 841-3200
www.cgi.ca

Chairman, CEO: Serge Godin
President, COO: Jean Brassard

Revenue Growth	★★★★★
Pre-tax Income Growth	★★★★★
Total Return	★★★★★
Return on Capital Employed	★★★★★
TSE: GIB.A	**20**

The boundaries between product supplier and service provider have blurred. Companies that sell hardware or software also want to offer integration and "e-business" consulting services. Meanwhile, customers are clearly indicating their desire to outsource their battles with the ever-morphing information technology (IT) monster. Couple this with the explosion of the Internet and you can begin to understand why CGI Group Inc. has been one of Canada's most consistent technology performers. Its independence from any particular hardware or software platform gives it an edge when competing with competing offerings from original equipment manufacturers (OEMs) seeking to be a one-stop shop.

CGI Group is the largest independent information technology services company in Canada, and the fifth-largest in North America. Headquartered in Montreal, the company employs over 8000 people.

The company derives its revenue from outsourcing of IT services, systems integration, and consulting. For fiscal 1999 (year ending September 30, 1999) these segments accounted for 72 percent, 17 percent, and 11 percent, respectively, of revenue worth $1.4 billion. This revenue figure marks a 90 percent increase versus fiscal 1998 and a 147 percent increase versus fiscal 1997. Overall, fiscal 1999 saw the twenty-third consecutive year of revenue growth for the company.

Outsourcing services include data and call centres, applications maintenance and support, and client-specific projects, including data warehousing and systems architecture. The company specializes in long-term, highly integrated contracts with clients that typically last for three to ten years.

The company reported a $7.5 billion order backlog at the end of fiscal 1999.

The company is divided into six strategic business units: Ontario and the Atlantic Provinces, Quebec, Western Canada, the United States, International, and Telecommunications. For fiscal 1999 81 percent of revenue was produced in Canada, 10 percent in the United States, and 9 percent overseas (mostly in Europe). The company's non-Americas business is conducted by a separately incorporated company, London, England–based Certis.

The Telecommunications unit accounted for 36 percent of revenue in 1999. The company also reports that 20 percent of its revenue is now derived from Web-based technologies. Note that BCE Inc. held a 45 percent equity interest in CGI Group at the end of fiscal 1999.

The company's shares are listed on the Toronto, Montreal, and New York stock exchanges.

Revenue Growth: ★★★★★

Past five years: 106 percent

Pre-tax Income Growth: ★★★★★

Past five years: 210 percent

Total Return: ★★★★★

Past five years: 159 percent

Return on Capital Employed: ★★★★★

Past five years: 28 percent

CGI Group Inc. at a Glance

Fiscal year ended: September 1999

Revenue and net income in $ millions

	1995	1996	1997	1998	1999	4-Year Growth Average (%)	4-Year Growth Total (%)
Total Revenue	97	122	232	741	1,409	106.49	1,357.71
Net Income	1	3	8	35	84	207.88	7,814.64
Earnings/ Share ($)	0.011	0.02	0.05	0.15	0.315	135.45	2,763.64
Dividend/ Share ($)	0	0	0	0	0	–	–
Dividend Yield (%)	0	0	0	0	0	–	–
Price to Earnings (PE)	12.73	21.1	95.5	76.33	46.03	–	–

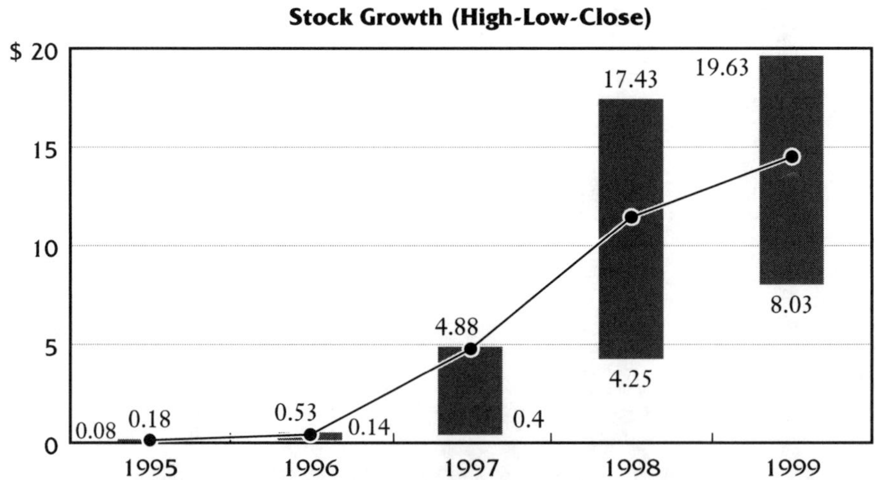

Close	0.14	0.42	4.78	11.45	14.5

5

FOUR SEASONS HOTELS INC.

1165 Leslie Street
Toronto, ON M3C 2K8
(416) 441-4329
www.fourseasons.com

Chairman, CEO: Isadore Sharp
President, COO: Wolf H. Hengst

Revenue Growth	★★★★★
Pre-tax Income Growth	★★★★★
Total Return	★★★★★
Return on Capital Employed	★★★★★
TSE: FSH	**20**

Four Seasons Hotels Inc. is a worldwide hotel and resort company. The company earns revenue from hotel and resort management and ownership, although since 1993 it has adopted a strategy of divesting itself of its ownership positions in order to concentrate on management. While most investors think of baby boomer stocks in terms of medical/pharmaceutical and financial services, many overlook the fact that as baby boomers start to hit their peak earning years (presently) they will have more disposable income beyond their RRSP contributions. A significant portion of this "excess" income will be spent on leisure time/travelling, which indicates that Four Seasons should remain a top financial performer. The company's long-term outlook is obviously strong given that retirees like to spend time away from home.

At the end of fiscal 1998 the company managed 43 hotel and resort properties in 18 countries in North America, Europe, Asia, Australia, and the Caribbean, generally under the Four Seasons and Regent banners. The company had ownership interests in or loans outstanding to 11 of those 43 properties. At the end of the first nine months of fiscal 1999 (ending September 30, 1999) the company reported management of 44 properties.

According to the company, its management agreements dictate that the hotel owner is responsible for the hotel's capital expenditures and requirements, including the salaries and benefits of hotel employees. Four Seasons provides day-to-day operational oversight, including hiring, training, purchasing, and budgeting. The company operates centralized reservations services and marketing for the Four Seasons brand, and centralized purchasing for both Four Seasons and some Regent properties.

Revenue for fiscal 1998 (year ending December 31, 1998) was $249 million, of which $123 million came from hotel management and $126 million came from hotel ownership. In fiscal 1997 revenue was $240 million, with management and ownership accounting for $106 million and $135 million, respectively.

For fiscal 1999, the company reported consolidated revenue of $277 million. Of this revenue, management accounted for $144 million and ownership accounted for $133 million.

Four Season Hotels Inc. is headquartered in Toronto and employs approximately 275 people directly worldwide; there are over 23,000 employees under its management at various hotels and resorts.

Four Seasons Hotels Inc. is listed on the Toronto, New York, and Montreal stock exchanges.

Revenue Growth: ★★★★★
Past five years: 26 percent

Pre-tax Income Growth: ★★★★★
Past five years: 68 percent

Total Return: ★★★★★
Past five years: 41 percent

Return on Capital Employed: ★★★★★
Past five years: 51 percent

Four Seasons Hotels Inc. at a Glance

Fiscal year ended: December 1999

Revenue and net income in $ millions

						4-Year Growth	
	1995	1996	1997	1998	1999	Average (%)	Total (%)
Total Revenue	136	121	240	249	278	25.81	104.7
Net Income	–75	30	41	70	86	67.9	215.97
Earnings/ Share ($)	–2.62	1.04	1.24	2.06	2.52	61.85	196.18
Dividend/ Share ($)	0.11	0.11	0.11	0.11	0.11	–	0
Dividend Yield (%)	0.58	0.4	0.24	0.24	0.14	–	–
Price to Earnings (PE)	N/A	26.68	36.29	21.84	30.48	–	–

Stock Growth (High-Low-Close)

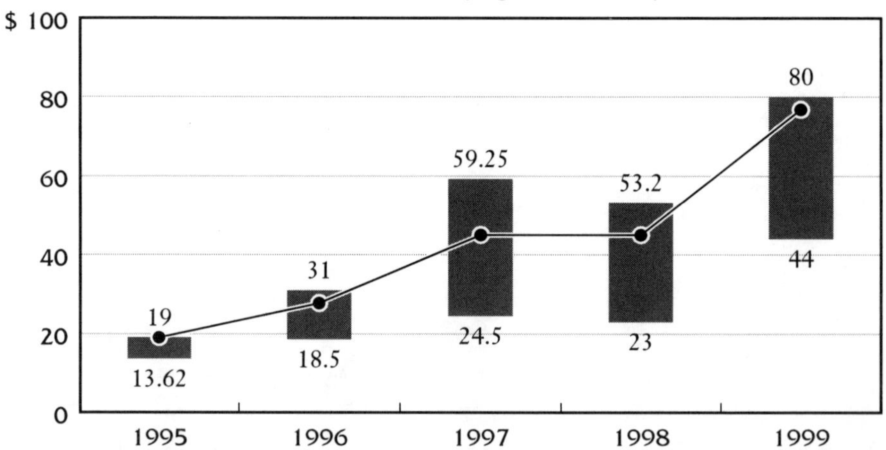

Close	19	27.75	45	45	76.8

6

COGNOS INC.

P.O. Box 9707, Station T
Ottawa, ON K1G 4K9
(613) 738-1440
www.cognos.com

President, CEO: Renato Zambonini

Revenue Growth	★★★★★
Pre-tax Income Growth	★★★★★
Total Return	★★★★★
Return on Capital Employed	★★★★★
TSE: CSN	**20**

Cognos Inc. is an information technology company that develops, licenses, and supports two major types of enterprise-level software for large and medium-sized corporations: business-intelligence software designed to allow individual users to analyze and manipulate corporate data, and application development tools for software developers. These products are distributed both through resellers and directly from Cognos.

While the company's growth has not been without volatility, Cognos continues to emerge as a leading supplier of software services to major corporations worldwide.

The company's revenue for fiscal 1999 (year ending February 28, 1999) was US$301 million (C$454 million). Of this, US$158 million (53 percent) came from product licensing (US$49 million of which was sold via third-party channels), US$93 million (31 percent) came from product support, and US$49 million (16 percent) came from product-related services such as training and consulting. Overall, revenue increased 23 percent versus fiscal 1998.

Cognos operates in three distinct geographic markets: the Americas (primarily North America), Europe, and Asia/Pacific. For fiscal 1999 these regions accounted for 59 percent, 34 percent, and 7 percent of revenue, respectively. The company's significant foreign revenue exposes it to fluctuations in currency exchange versus the U.S. dollar (the company's currency for accounting purposes); Cognos hedges portions of its foreign-currency contracts in order to minimize this risk.

The company spent over US$42 million on research and development in fiscal 1999; this represents approximately 14 percent of revenue. Cognos has been increasingly active in the development of Web- and intranet-based products.

Cognos has recently acquired several companies with compatible products, including: Relational Matters, which makes data manipulation software, in December 1998; and LEX2000 Inc., which makes financial reporting software, in February 1999. In November 1998 Cognos purchased Business Intelligence University, an executive training course that focuses on organizational decision making.

Cognos is based in Ottawa and employs over 1600 people.

Revenue Growth: ★★★★★
Past five years: 28 percent

Pre-tax Income Growth: ★★★★★
Past five years: 67 percent

Total Return: ★★★★★
Past five years: 57 percent

Return on Capital Employed: ★★★★★
Past five years: 22 percent

Cognos Inc. at a Glance

Fiscal year ended: February 2000

Revenue and net income in US$ millions

	1995	1996	1997	1998	1999	4-Year Growth Average (%)	4-Year Growth Total (%)
Total Revenue	169	209	271	349	454	28	168.18
Net Income	11	24	50	46	88	75.5	672.26
Earnings/ Share ($)	0.278	0.548	1.094	1.011	1.975	71.13	610.43
Dividend/ Share ($)	0	0	0	0	0	–	–
Dividend Yield (%)	0	0	0	0	0	–	–
Price to Earnings (PE)	35.37	42.88	29.25	36.6	15.7	–	–

Stock Growth (High-Low-Close)

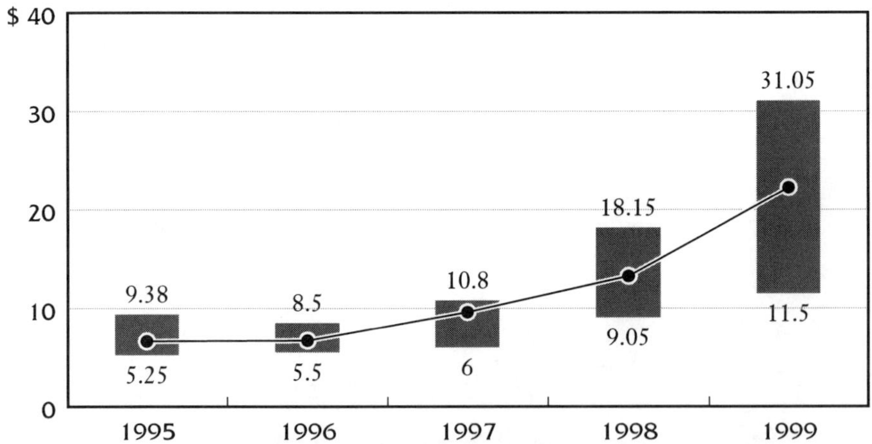

	1995	1996	1997	1998	1999
Close	6.63	6.7	9.6	13.25	22.25

7

McGRAW-HILL RYERSON LTD.

300 Water Street
Whitby, ON L1N 9B6
(905) 430-5000
www.mcgrawhill.ca

President, CEO: John D. Dill

Revenue Growth	★★★★
Pre-tax Income Growth	★★★★★
Total Return	★★★★★
Return on Capital Employed	★★★★★
TSE: MHR	**19**

McGraw-Hill Ryerson Ltd. is a print and non-print media publisher of educational, professional, and trade materials. Although much smaller in terms of revenue than a lot of the companies profiled in this book, McGraw-Hill is probably better known than many of them. Like some of the other media/publishing companies we have profiled, the advent of the Internet brings these companies' assets into new focus.

For fiscal 1999 (year ending December 31, 1999) the company reported revenue of $77 million, versus $68 million in the previous year, a 13 percent increase. This was the company's fifth consecutive year of growth.

McGraw-Hill Ryerson's business is segmented into three revenue divisions to address different markets: Higher Education (universities and community colleges), School (secondary schools, elementary schools, and career colleges), and Trade, Professional, and Medical (booksellers, book distributors, libraries, and direct sales).

In fiscal 1998 these three divisions accounted for 50 percent, 28 percent, and 22 percent of revenue, respectively.

In 1998 the company created the Lifelong Learning Marketing Group to sell training materials, particularly those with multimedia or online components, to governments and corporations.

McGraw-Hill Companies Inc., a U.S. firm, owns approximately 70 percent of McGraw-Hill Ryerson's outstanding shares. McGraw-Hill Ryerson operates independently, publishing under and distributing a number of imprints.

The information age has placed a premium on the technology that packages and delivers all those megabytes. Lately, the acquisition of media companies by cable companies (for example, Rogers' purchase of Maclean Hunter), Internet service providers (AOL's acquisition of Time Warner) and telephone companies (Bell's bid for CTV) has highlighted the value of publishing concerns and content providers. Companies such as McGraw-Hill with unique libraries will be attractive to those looking to diversify their content base away from pure entertainment into the education and professional fields. This should provide McGraw-Hill with new growth in revenues and other strategic opportunities.

McGraw-Hill Ryerson Ltd. is based in Whitby, Ontario, and employs approximately 180 people.

Revenue Growth: ★★★★

Past five years: 19 percent

Pre-tax Income Growth: ★★★★★

Past five years: 59 percent

Total Return: ★★★★★

Past five years: 22 percent

Return on Capital Employed: ★★★★★

Past five years: 42 percent

McGraw-Hill Ryerson Ltd. at a Glance

Fiscal year ended: December 1999

Revenue and net income in $ millions

						4-Year Growth	
	1995	1996	1997	1998	1999	Average (%)	Total (%)
Total Revenue	39	44	62	68	77	19.59	100.79
Net Income	2	2	4	5	6	51.04	260.6
Earnings/ Share ($)	0.81	0.81	2.23	2.61	2.93	51.15	261.73
Dividend/ Share ($)	0.2	0.2	0.2	0.4	0.5	31.25	150
Dividend Yield (%)	2.32	1.82	1.14	1.82	2.2	–	–
Price to Earnings (PE)	10.65	13.58	7.85	8.43	7.76	–	–

Stock Growth (High-Low-Close)

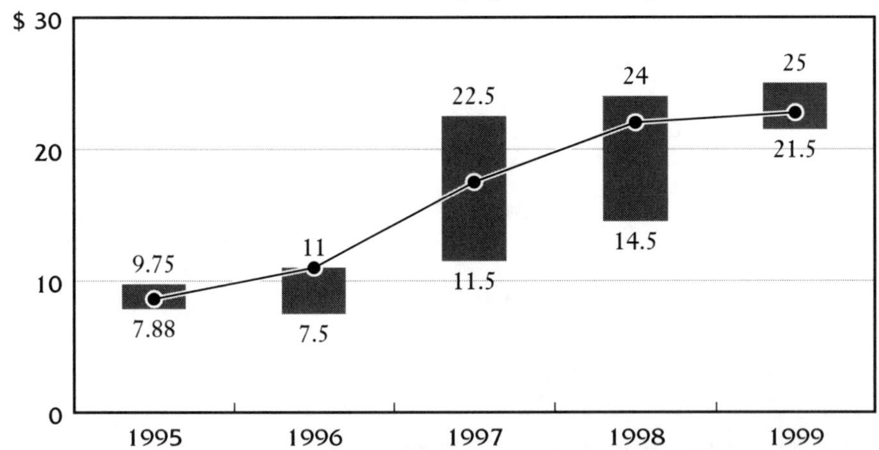

Close	8.62	11	17.5	22	22.75

8

INTRAWEST CORP.

200 Burrard Street, Suite 800
Vancouver, BC V6C 3L6
(604) 623-6626
www.intrawest.com

President, Chairman, CEO: J.S. Houssian

Revenue Growth	★★★★★
Pre-tax Income Growth	★★★★★
Total Return	★★★★
Return on Capital Employed	★★★★★
TSE: ITW	**19**

Vancouver-based Intrawest is a mountain-resort developer and operator with ten mountain resorts across North America, including Whistler/Blackcomb in British Columbia and Tremblant in Quebec. Altogether, the company's resorts attracted approximately 6.4 million visitors during the 1998–99 winter season. Intrawest is also North America's largest mountain-resort real estate developer, developing and managing commercial and residential properties at each of its resorts. Part hotel operator, part real estate developer, part leisure service provider, Intrawest's unique blend of business positions it to take advantage of the current and increasing growth in baby boomer travel.

Intrawest also owns equity positions in France's Compagnie des Alpes, the world's largest ski operator (in terms of ski visits), and Alpine Helicopters Ltd., the parent company of Canadian Mountain Holidays, the world's largest heli-skiing operation. In 1998, the company also acquired Colorado-based ski and snowboard equipment rental companies Breeze, Inc. and Max Snowboard, Inc.

The company has also begun to expand into warm-weather resorts, acquiring in 1998 Sandestin Resorts Inc., a Florida golf and beach resort and residential community, and the assets of the Raven Golf Group, including two resort-quality golf courses in Arizona.

In fiscal 1999 (year ending June 30, 1999) the company reported revenue of $921 million (versus $602 million in fiscal 1998), of which ski and resort operations accounted for $578 million (versus $367 million) and real estate operations accounted for $334 million (versus $231 million). Other sources of revenue accounted for $9 million in 1999 and $4 million in 1998.

For the first six months of fiscal 2000 (ended December 31, 1999) Intrawest reported US$272 million in revenue, a 68 percent increase over the same period in the previous year.

Intrawest is a prime example of the way that a company can bring aggressive new business ideas to bear on mature industries to create unique products and services that specifically appeal to baby boomers.

Intrawest is listed on the Toronto, Montreal, and New York stock exchanges.

Revenue Growth: ★★★★★

Past five years: 58 percent

Pre-tax Income Growth: ★★★★★

Past five years: 59 percent

Total Return: ★★★★

Past five years: 18 percent

Return on Capital Employed: ★★★★★

Past five years: 20 percent

Intrawest Corp. at a Glance

Fiscal year ended: June 1999

Revenue and net income in $ millions

						4-Year Growth	
	1995	1996	1997	1998	1999	Average (%)	Total (%)
Total Revenue	153	283	389	602	921	57.57	502.06
Net Income	12	18	27	41	51	45.17	338.22
Earnings/ Share ($)	0.51	0.76	1.05	1.19	1.28	27.02	150.98
Dividend/ Share ($)	0.16	0.16	0.16	0.16	0.16	–	0
Dividend Yield (%)	1.36	1.11	0.7	0.55	0.71	–	–
Price to Earnings (PE)	23.04	19.01	21.86	24.58	17.66	–	–

Stock Growth (High-Low-Close)

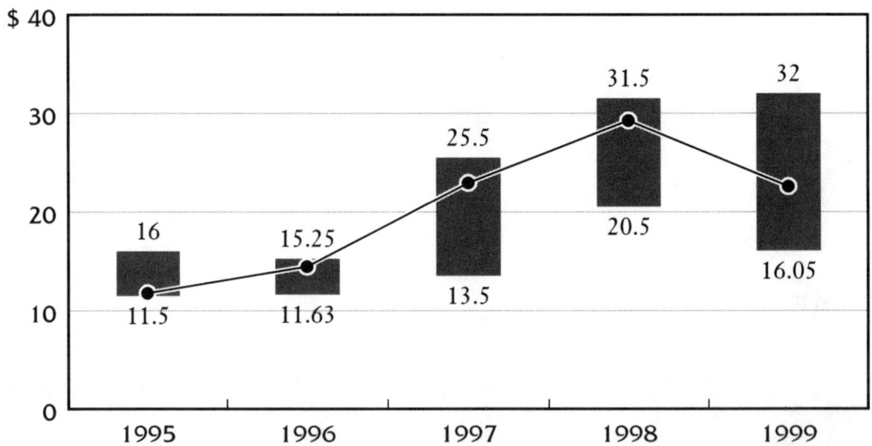

	1995	1996	1997	1998	1999
Close	11.75	14.45	22.95	29.25	22.6

9

TORONTO DOMINION BANK

P.O. Box 1, Toronto-Dominion Centre
Toronto, ON M5K 1A2
(416) 982-8222
www.tdbank.ca

Chairman, CEO: A.C. Baillie

Revenue Growth	★★★★
Pre-tax Income Growth	★★★★★
Total Return	★★★★★
Return on Capital Employed	★★★★★
TSE: TD	**19**

No surprises here. When most Canadians think of blue-chip stocks, they think of the big banks. And of the bunch, it's hard to beat TD Bank. What sets this bank apart is its entrepreneurial drive and innovation. In an industry where innovation seems to proceed at a perpetually glacial pace, TD vaults from one new idea to another. It is no wonder that it was the first of the "big five" (Royal Bank, Bank of Montreal, CIBC, ScotiaBank and TD) to enter the brokerage business and one of the most aggressive in rolling out ATM machines.

And the list goes on. This innovation has also meant a financial performance that has consistently seen TD Bank generate the best returns on shareholders' equity despite being the smallest of Canada's "big five" banks.

Toronto Dominion Bank was created in 1955 from the union of the Bank of Toronto and the Dominion Bank. TD Bank was ranked fourth among Canadian banks in terms of market capitalization as of October 31, 1998, with total assets of $181.8 billion.

TD Bank Financial Group, which includes TD Bank and all of its affiliated companies, employs more than 32,000 people, with over 1000 retail banking and investment outlets across Canada, the United States, and various world financial capitals such as Hong Kong, London, Mexico City, and Tokyo.

Personal banking services offered by TD Bank include savings and chequing accounts, term deposits, mutual funds, mortgage loans, and a range of Visa credit cards. Business and corporate banking services include term lending, commercial deposits, leasing, international monetary transfers, and a wide range of financial advisory services.

TD Bank's wholesale investment dealer is TD Securities, which provides financial services in four areas: investment banking, equities, debt capital markets, and foreign exchange. TD Bank's full-service investment brokerage and wealth-management firm is TD Evergreen. TD Waterhouse Group, TD Bank's discount brokerage (including online trading), trades separately on the New York and Toronto stock exchanges.

Investors always ask which bank is the best. This is a hard question to answer, and it really boils down to personal bias, as each bank has its different strengths. In the case of TD Bank, we come back to its strengths as an innovator and its unparalleled record of above-industry-average profitability.

Revenue Growth: ★★★★

Past five years: 16 percent

Pre-tax Income Growth: ★★★★★

Past five years: 28 percent

Total Return: ★★★★★

Past five years: 24 percent

Return on Capital Employed: ★★★★★

Past five years: 5 percent

Toronto Dominion Bank at a Glance

Fiscal year ended: October 1999

Revenue and net income in $ millions

	1995	1996	1997	1998	1999	4-Year Growth Average (%)	4-Year Growth Total (%)
Total Revenue	8,727	9,071	10,476	13,194	15,683	16.06	79.71
Net Income	794	914	1,088	1,121	2,981	50.78	275.44
Earnings/ Share ($)	1.255	1.475	1.77	1.81	4.9	52.63	290.44
Dividend/ Share ($)	0.44	0.5	0.56	0.66	0.72	13.15	63.64
Dividend Yield (%)	3.71	3.19	2.17	2.88	2.13	–	–
Price to Earnings (PE)	9.46	10.63	14.59	12.68	6.89	–	–

Stock Growth (High-Low-Close)

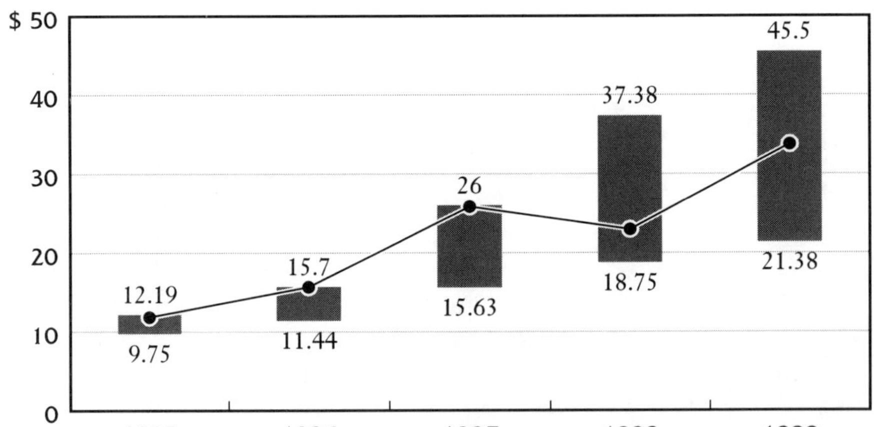

Close	11.88	15.68	25.83	22.95	33.75

10

COGECO INC.

1 Place Ville Marie, Suite 3636
Montreal, PQ H3B 2P2
(514) 874-2600
www.cogeco.com

President, CEO: Louis Audet

Revenue Growth	★★★★
Pre-tax Income Growth	★★★★★
Total Return	★★★★★
Return on Capital Employed	★★★★★
TSE: CGO	**19**

Montreal-based COGECO is a communications company with two major sectors: the cable sector, consisting of the company's 46.8 percent ownership of its subsidiary, the publicly traded Cogeco Cable Inc.; and the media sector, consisting of the wholly owned subsidiary Cogeco Radio-Television Inc. (CRTI). The company employs over 1200 people.

Cogeco Cable Inc.'s September 1999 acquisition of Cableworks Communications Inc. raised the company's total number of basic cable subscribers to over 830,000, making Cogeco Cable the fourth-largest cable operator in Canada. Approximately 70 percent of these subscribers are in Ontario; the rest are in Quebec. The company has now divested itself of all of its cable assets in western Canada.

As of the end of fiscal 1999 Cogeco Cable had laid out over 50,000 kilometres of fibre-optic cable to complete a network covering 3200 kilometres from Windsor, Ontario, to Campbellton, New Brunswick.

The company has undergone considerable technical modifications of its cable system so as to make itself ready for high-speed Internet access and telephony. COGECO is currently in the middle of a program to replace existing analog equipment with digital technology. The end result will be a six- to tenfold increase in video bandwidth, allowing for future expansion into video-on-demand and Internet-TV services.

Fiscal 1999 revenue for COGECO's cable sector was $325.4 million, a 13 percent increase over fiscal 1998.

CRTI owns and operates six French-language television stations and two French-language radio stations in Quebec. CRTI also owns a production company, Les Productions Carrefour Inc., which produces French-language programs.

Fiscal 1999 revenue for COGECO's media sector was $33.5 million, versus $29.3 million in fiscal 1998.

While COGECO is certainly not the largest cable concern in Canada, the growth in demands on broadband networks should ensure that the "pie" continues to grow for all well-run operators. With its diverse telecommunications assets, COGECO remains a top pick in this sector. COGECO is listed on the Montreal and Toronto stock exchanges.

Revenue Growth: ★★★★
Past five years: 15 percent

Pre-tax Income Growth: ★★★★★
Past five years: 73 percent

Total Return: ★★★★★
Past five years: 45 percent

Return on Capital Employed: ★★★★★
Past five years: 23 percent

COGECO Inc. at a Glance

Fiscal year ended: August 1999

Revenue and net income in $ millions

	1995	1996	1997	1998	1999	4-Year Growth Average (%)	4-Year Growth Total (%)
Total Revenue	207	215	275	316	359	15.07	73.46
Net Income	5	8	18	20	53	90.28	960
Earnings/ Share ($)	0.29	0	1.09	1.23	3.21	–	1,006.9
Dividend/ Share ($)	0.115	0.12	0.16	0.2	0.21	16.92	82.61
Dividend Yield (%)	1.74	1.79	1.67	1.51	0.94	–	–
Price to Earnings (PE)	22.84	N/A	8.81	10.77	6.93	–	–

Stock Growth (High-Low-Close)

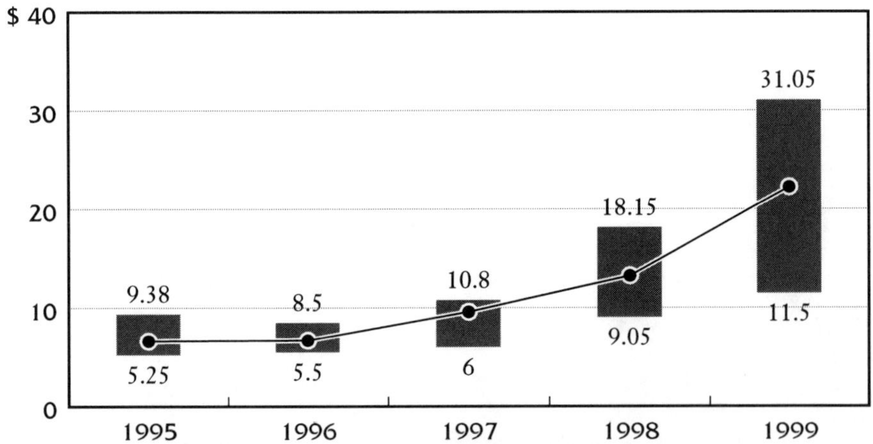

Close	6.63	6.7	9.6	13.25	22.25

11

ONEX CORP.

161 Bay Street, P.O. Box 700
Toronto, ON M5J 2S1
(416) 362-7711
www.onexcorp.com

Chairman & CEO: Gerald W. Schwartz

Revenue Growth	★★★★★
Pre-tax Income Growth	★★★★★
Total Return	★★★★★
Return on Capital Employed	★★★★
TSE: OCX	**19**

Onex Corp. is a diversified global company with subsidiaries in a wide variety of businesses, including airline catering, electronics, automotive components, marketing services, sugar processing, entertainment, and venture capital. Some recent failed acquisitions (Labatt and Air Canada) have taken some of the lustre away from Onex's other very successful investments. Time and time again Onex has been able to make significant investment in businesses and, through shrewd management, magnify the value of those investments. In some cases Onex has been able to realize gains within a few months of initial investment.

More specifically, the company's principal subsidiaries are:

- LSG Sky Chefs, the largest in-flight caterer in the world (Onex ownership: 44 percent; voting: 53 percent, as of December 31, 1998).
- Celestica, the world's third-largest electronics manufacturing services provider (ownership: 22 percent; voting: 88 percent).
- ClientLogic, a marketing-services provider with clients across North America and Europe (ownership: 83 percent; voting: 100 percent).
- Hidden Creek Industries, which operates a number of automotive component suppliers (ownership: 90 percent).
- American Buildings Company, a manufacturer and marketer of engineered metal products for mainly non-residential construction (ownership: 54 percent).
- Lantic Sugar, Canada's largest sugar refiner and marketer (ownership: 61 percent; voting: 75 percent).
- Phoenix Pictures, an entertainment company (ownership: 26 percent).
- Vencap, a venture capital fund (ownership: 90 percent; voting: 100 percent).

For fiscal 1999 (year ending December 31, 1999) the company reported consolidated revenue of $14.9 billion, versus $8.8 billion in fiscal 1998, a 69 percent increase.

As mentioned earlier, during 1999 Onex was at the centre of a highly publicized attempt to acquire both Air Canada and Canadian Airlines and merge them into a single carrier. Although it did not succeed in that attempt, Onex did, through its subsidiaries, complete approximately $5 billion worth of acquisitions in 1999.

In June 1999 the company's stock split two for one.

Onex Corporation is headquartered in Toronto and employs approximately 83,000 people worldwide through its various subsidiaries.

Revenue Growth: ★★★★★

Past five years: 71 percent

Pre-tax Income Growth: ★★★★★

Past five years: 65 percent

Total Return: ★★★★★

Past five years: 47 percent

Return on Capital Employed: ★★★★

Past five years: 19 percent

Onex Corp. at a Glance

Fiscal year ended: December 1999

Revenue and net income in $ millions

	1995	1996	1997	1998	1999	4-Year Growth Average (%)	4-Year Growth Total (%)
Total Revenue	1,765	3,232	5,811	8,813	14,869	70.81	742.24
Net Income	77	87	54	177	294	66.57	281.21
Earnings/ Share ($)	1.035	1.145	0.62	1.955	3.34	62.64	222.71
Dividend/ Share ($)	0.218	0.22	0.22	0.22	0.22	0.23	0.92
Dividend Yield (%)	2.93	2.26	1.54	1.01	0.42	–	–
Price to Earnings (PE)	7.19	8.52	23.06	11.13	15.64	–	–

Stock Growth (High-Low-Close)

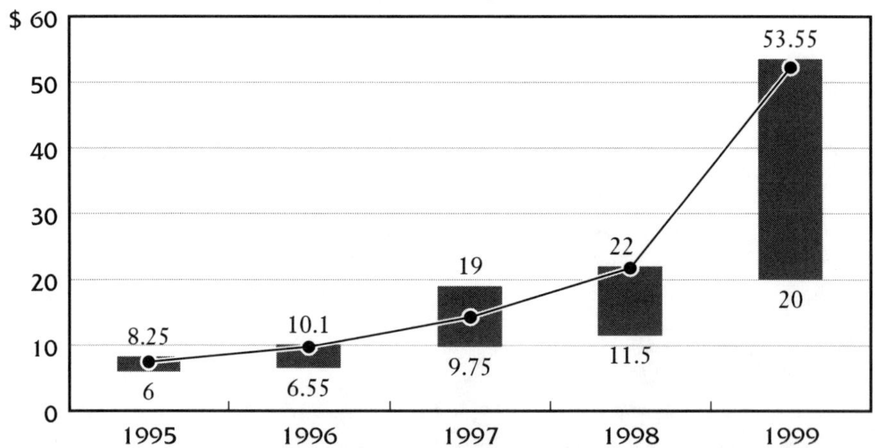

Close	7.44	9.75	14.3	21.75	52.25

12

RIO ALTO EXPLORATION LTD.

205, 5th Avenue SW, Suite 2500
Calgary, AB T2P 2V7
(403) 264-8780
www.rioalto.com

President, CFO: Richard T. Cones

Revenue Growth	★★★★★
Pre-tax Income Growth	★★★★★
Total Return	★★★★★
Return on Capital Employed	★★★★
TSE: RAX	**19**

Calgary-based Rio Alto Exploration Ltd. is involved in petroleum and natural gas exploration, development, production, and sales.

Besides the company's strong record of exploration success, it has also grown through strategic acquisitions and by maintaining operating control over a number of its assets. With a keen eye on its expense and cost control, Rio Alto is particularly well positioned to leverage the higher commodity prices of the past few years.

The company's sizeable land holdings and reserves augur well for the future. By sticking with similar geological and geographic boundaries over the years, the company has been able to mitigate some of the inherent risk in exploring for oil and natural gas.

Average daily production of the company's properties, as of December 31, 1999, was 7860 barrels of oil and liquids and 365 million cubic feet of natural gas. The company reported reserves (proved and probable) of more than 53 million barrels of oil and liquids and over 1.5 trillion cubic feet of natural gas. The company also reported over 2.5 million acres of gross undeveloped land, with an average working interest of 90 percent.

In fiscal 1999 (year ending December 31, 1999) the company had revenue of $316 million, versus $208 million in 1998, an increase of 52 percent.

During fiscal 1999 the company drilled or participated in the drilling of 110 wells, with an average success rate of 76 percent.

Rio Alto employs approximately 250 people.

Revenue Growth: ★★★★★

Past five years: 49 percent

Pre-tax Income Growth: ★★★★★

Past five years: 90 percent

Total Return: ★★★★★

Past five years: 43 percent

Return on Capital Employed: ★★★★

Past five years: 15 percent

Rio Alto Exploration Ltd. at a Glance

Fiscal year ended: December 1999

Revenue and net income in $ millions

	1995	1996	1997	1998	1999	4-Year Growth Average (%)	4-Year Growth Total (%)
Total Revenue	64	101	152	208	316	49.11	391.97
Net Income	8	23	36	37	70	84.53	786.62
Earnings/ Share ($)	0.18	0.48	0.68	0.6	1.03	67.06	472.22
Dividend/ Share ($)	0	0	0	0	0	–	–
Dividend Yield (%)	0	0	0	0	0	–	–
Price to Earnings (PE)	29.86	20.73	17.65	25	19.81	–	–

Stock Growth (High-Low-Close)

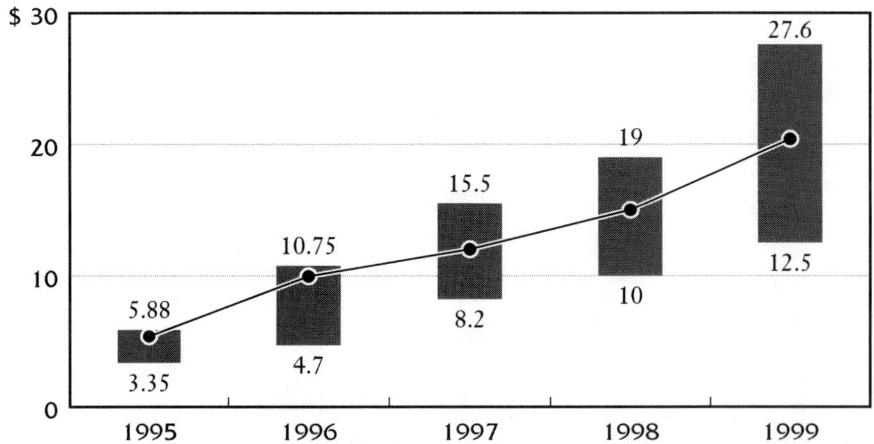

Close	5.38	9.95	12	15	20.4

13

CORBY DISTILLERIES LTD.

193 Yonge Street
Toronto, ON M5B 1M8
(416) 369-1859
www.corby.ca

President, CEO: Krystyna T. Hoeg

Revenue Growth	★★★★★
Pre-tax Income Growth	★★★★★
Total Return	★★★★
Return on Capital Employed	★★★★★
TSE: CDL.A	**19**

The ultimate recession company, Corby Distilleries is the number-one manufacturer and marketer of spirits in Canada. It is also the country's leading wine importer. We say that it's the ultimate recession company because even economic downturns appear to do little to alter the pattern of alcohol consumption!

The company's value is a result of its broad range of recognized spirits brands, both owned and represented. The company sells 9 of the top 25 brands in Canada, including Canadian Club, Canada's best-selling Canadian whisky.

Overall, in fiscal 1999 (year ending August 31, 1999) Corby owned a 47 percent share of the tequila market, 42.5 percent of the Canadian whisky market, 33 percent of the liqueur market, 33 percent of the gin market, 24 percent of the brandy and cognac market, 21 percent of the rum market, 14 percent of the scotch whisky market, and 11 percent of the vodka market.

Brands of spirits owned or represented by Corby include Sauza, Wiser's De Luxe, Ballantine's, Teacher's, Kahlua, Courvoisier, Drambuie, Hennessy, Lamb's, Polar Ice, and Beefeater.

Corby shipped 1.1 million cases of wine in fiscal 1999. Represented labels include Freixenet (Canada's number-one-selling imported sparkling wine), as well as Dom Perignon and Moët & Chandon. The company views the wine business, particularly New World wines, to be a tremendous opportunity (leveraging the company's existing spirits sales and distribution infrastructure), and in fiscal 1999 created the management position of Director of Wines.

Revenue for fiscal 1999 was $101 million, versus $97 million in fiscal 1998. The company's sales are predominantly in Canada, although export opportunities to the United States and Europe are in development.

The company moved its head office from Montreal to Toronto (where 20 percent of its sales take place) during fiscal 1998.

Hiram Walker and Sons Ltd., a wholly owned subsidiary of Allied Domecq PLC, owns more than 50 percent of Corby's issued common voting shares.

As already suggested, consumer products stocks such as Corby's are less vulnerable to the vagaries of economic cycles and, as such, prove to be relatively defensive investments. And it's fun to own a part of Canada's whisky heritage.

Revenue Growth: ★★★★★

Past five years: 32 percent

Pre-tax Income Growth: ★★★★★

Past five years: 26 percent

Total Return: ★★★★

Past five years: 19 percent

Return on Capital Employed: ★★★★★

Past five years: 30 percent

Corby Distilleries Ltd. at a Glance

Fiscal year ended: August 1999

Revenue and net income in $ millions

	1995	1996	1997	1998	1999	4-Year Growth Average (%)	4-Year Growth Total (%)
Total Revenue	41	84	92	97	101	31.61	148.68
Net Income	12	27	29	28	23	25.42	83.86
Earnings/ Share ($)	1.75	3.77	4.06	3.98	3.25	25.7	85.71
Dividend/ Share ($)	0.62	1.24	1.28	18.2	2	334.02	222.58
Dividend Yield (%)	1.64	2.88	2.33	24.93	2.86	–	–
Price to Earnings (PE)	21.57	11.41	13.55	18.34	21.54	–	–

Stock Growth (High-Low-Close)

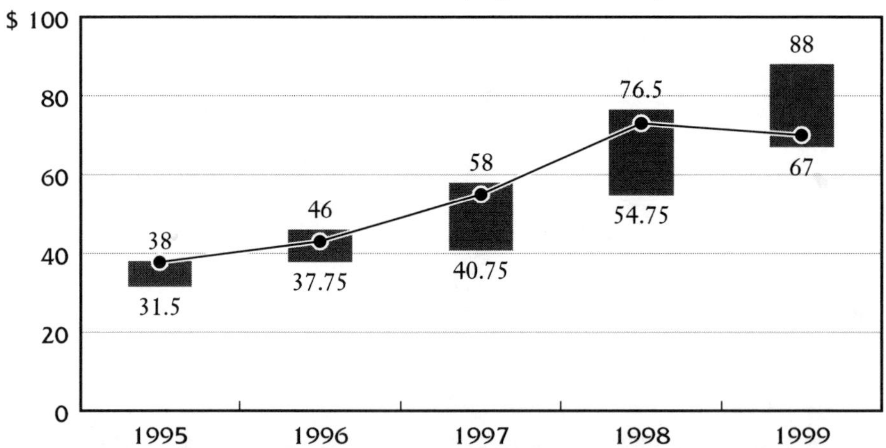

Close	37.75	43	55	73	70

14

NOVA CHEMICALS CORP.

645 Seventh Avenue SW Box 2518
Calgary, AB T2P 5C6
(403) 750-3600
www.novachem.com

President, CEO: J.M. Lipton

Revenue Growth	★ ★ ★
Pre-tax Income Growth	★ ★ ★ ★ ★
Total Return	★ ★ ★ ★ ★
Return on Capital Employed	★ ★ ★ ★ ★
TSE: NCX	**18**

NOVA Chemicals Corporation is the largest petrochemical company in Canada. The company manufactures two primary types of commodity chemicals: olefins/polyolefins (such as ethylene and polyethylene) and styrenics (such as styrene and polystyrene).These chemicals are the basic building blocks for plastics. They are used in the manufacturing of such industrial and consumer products as packaging and containers, plastic pipe, electronics, and appliances. The company also holds an approximately 27 percent interest in Methanex Corporation, the world's largest producer of methanol.

NOVA has gone through many changes over the years, the most significant being the spinoff of its gas pipeline business in the early 1990s. While very much a company whose fortunes rise and fall with the overall economy and commodity prices, NOVA has usually managed to outperform its peer group. This is a result of being among the lowest cost producers in a number of its product categories. It is, for example, the world's lowest cost producer of methanol, whose use should greatly expand should fuel cells ever take off. Through the last five years, NOVA has generated a modest average annual revenue increase but has coupled that with an almost 30 percent average growth in pre-tax income, while keeping a tight lid on costs.

Revenue for fiscal 1999 (year ending December 31, 1999) was US$2.8 billion, versus US$2.1 billion in fiscal 1998. For the first quarter of fiscal 2000 (ending March 31, 2000), the company reported revenue of US$521 million, versus US$477 million for the same period a year earlier.

Geographically, fiscal 1999 revenue was divided as follows: United States, 53%; Canada, 33%; Europe and elsewhere, 14%.

The company has operations in Canada, the United States, and Europe. In January 2000, the company completed the acquisition of the Royal Dutch/Shell Group's European polystyrene assets and sales operations for approximately US$210 million.

The company is headquartered in Calgary and, as of February 2000, employed approximately 4,700 people worldwide.

Revenue Growth: ★ ★ ★

Past five years: 14 percent

Pre-tax Income Growth: ★ ★ ★ ★ ★

Past five years: 194 percent

Total Return: ★ ★ ★ ★ ★

Past five years: 373 percent

Return on Capital Employed: ★ ★ ★ ★ ★

Past five years: 77 percent

NOVA Chemicals Corp. at a Glance

Fiscal year ended: December 1999

Revenue and net income in US$ millions

						3-Year Growth	
	1995	1996	1997	1998	1999	Average (%)	Total (%)
Total Revenue	–	2,836	3,269	3,176	4,081	13.64	43.91
Net Income	–	210	159	28	368	375.91	75.34
Earnings/ Share ($)	–	2.275	1.731	0.26	3.183	338.45	39.91
Dividend/ Share ($)	–	0.603	1.688	0.199	0.581	94.56	–3.65
Dividend Yield (%)	–	4.94	12.32	0.99	2.06	–	–
Price to Earnings (PE)	–	5.36	7.91	76.92	8.88	–	–

Stock Growth (High-Low-Close)

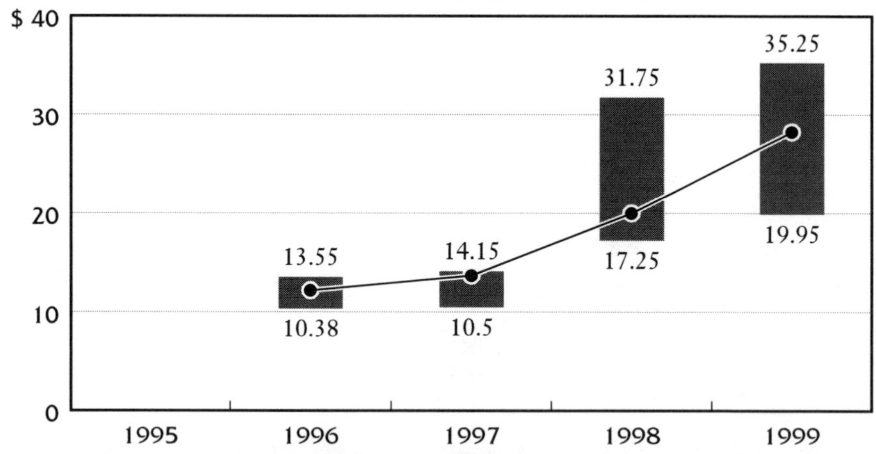

	1995	1996	1997	1998	1999
Close		12.2	13.7	20	28.25

15

SHAW COMMUNICATIONS INC.

630, 3rd Avenue SW, Suite 900
Calgary, AB T2P 4L4
(403) 750-4500
www.shaw.ca

Executive Chair: James R. Shaw, Sr.
President, CEO: Jim Shaw, Jr.

Revenue Growth	★★★
Pre-tax Income Growth	★★★★★
Total Return	★★★★★
Return on Capital Employed	★★★★★
TSE: SJR.B	**18**

Shaw Communications Inc. is a diversified communications and broadcast-media company that provides cable-television, telecommunications, high-speed Internet access, and satellite services. Like cross-country rival Rogers Communications, Shaw is rushing headlong into embracing new technology and rolling out the means to take advantage of the huge increase in demands on broadband systems.

The company's main business is cable-television services. Shaw has 1.8 million cable-television subscribers across seven provinces, making it the second-largest cable-television company in Canada. The company also has 185,000 Internet-access subscribers.

Shaw Communications owns approximately 35 percent of Canadian Satellite Communications Inc., which provides a range of satellite programming and services to both business and residential customers.

Shaw Communications' other businesses have been going through a period of tremendous change:

- The company's telecommunications subsidiary, Shaw Fibrelink, which provides businesses with fibre-optic Internet, data, voice, and video networking services, merged with GT Group Telecom Inc. Future operations will be conducted by GT Group Telecom, with Shaw receiving $360 million and a 28.5 percent ownership position in the company. This deal closed in February 2000.
- In November 1999 the company sold the assets and operations of Shaw Mobilecomm, a subsidiary that supplied paging services, to Rogers Cantel. Shaw will become a reseller of Cantel digital cellular telephone services.
- The company's radio-broadcasting and specialty-television programming assets (such as YTV Canada, Treehouse TV, and an 80 percent ownership of Country Music Television) were consolidated into a new, publicly traded company, Corus Entertainment Inc., in September 1999. In early 2000 Corus Entertainment was set to merge with radio-station and television programming assets acquired by Shaw in late 1999 from WIC Western International Communications Inc., pending approval from WIC's financial advisers.

The company reported revenue for fiscal 1999 (year ending August 31, 1999) of $728 million, versus $646 million in fiscal 1998.

First-quarter revenue for fiscal 2000 (three months ending November 30, 1999) was reported at $212 million, versus $165 million for the same period one year earlier.

Shaw Communications is headquartered in Calgary and employs 3200 people.

In February 2000 the company's shares underwent a two-for-one split.

Shares of Shaw Communications are traded on the Toronto, Alberta, and New York stock exchanges.

Revenue Growth: ★★★

Past five years: 14.6 percent

Pre-tax Income Growth: ★★★★★

Past five years: 110 percent

Total Return: ★★★★★

Past five years: 54 percent

Return on Capital Employed: ★★★★★

Past five years: 21 percent

Shaw Communications Inc. at a Glance

Fiscal year ended: August 1999

Revenue and net income in $ millions

	1995	1996	1997	1998	1999	4-Year Growth Average (%)	4-Year Growth Total (%)
Total Revenue	439	611	688	646	728	14.64	66.07
Net Income	29	64	17	14	46	65.88	56.15
Earnings/ Share ($)	0.225	0.455	0.12	–0.005	0.115	581.11	–48.89
Dividend/ Share ($)	0.035	0.035	0.035	0.04	0.04	3.57	14.29
Dividend Yield (%)	0.9	0.79	0.58	0.3	0.15	–	–
Price to Earnings (PE)	17.22	9.78	50.42	N/A	229.57	–	–

Stock Growth (High-Low-Close)

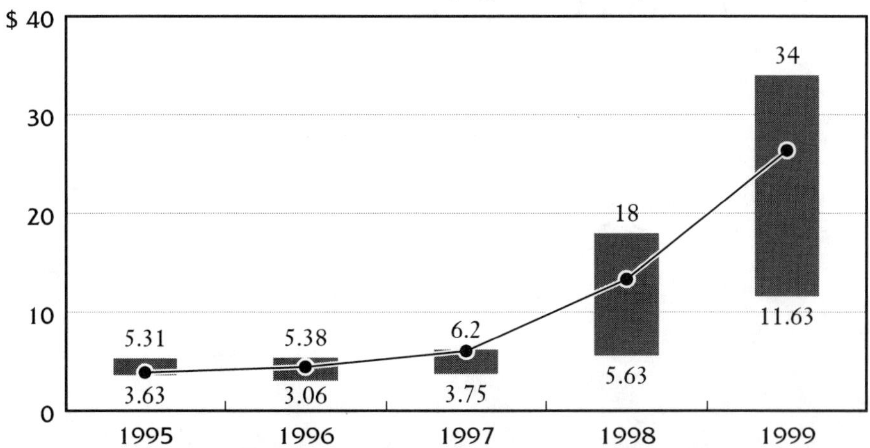

	1995	1996	1997	1998	1999
Close	3.88	4.45	6.05	13.35	26.4

16

AGF MANAGEMENT LTD.

P.O. Box 50
Toronto, ON M5K 1E9
(416) 367-1900
www.agf.com

Chairman, CEO: C.W. Goldring
President, COO: B.C. Goldring

Revenue Growth	★★★★★
Pre-tax Income Growth	★★★★★
Total Return	★★★★★
Return on Capital Employed	★★
TSE: AGF.B	**18**

AGF is one of those companies that fit into a theme—in this case the increasing wealth of the baby boom generation. While we are not necessarily fans of mutual funds from a personal investment viewpoint, the companies that own and manage these funds wield incredible marketing clout. Because of this and the fact that most people still are uncomfortable about managing their money without professional help, wealth management companies appear destined for sustained growth for some time to come.

AGF Management is one of Canada's oldest wealth-management companies. Founded in 1957, the company takes its name from the American Growth Fund, the first U.S. equity fund available to Canadian investors.

AGF offers a range of investment products and manages assets of over $17 billion for over 700,000 clients.

Headquartered in Toronto, the company has sales offices in Halifax, Montreal, and Vancouver, as well as portfolio management offices in Dublin and Singapore. The company employs over 700 people.

AGF and companies like it also have a major operating advantage over other types of companies, including other financial institutions: They can alter their asset and cost structure very quickly. If markets turn down, portfolios can be quickly liquidated and repositioned (this is not so easy with real estate or other hard assets). Most of AGF's sales force are "hired guns," that is, independent brokers and mutual fund sales representatives who aren't on the company payroll: They get paid when they sell. Thus corporate overhead is limited to a modest head office staff that includes some portfolio managers and analysts and a generous dose of marketing and client service types. Again, most of these employees are compensated largely for performance.

Because of these structural advantages and a fee regime generally more lucrative than that in the U.S., AGF outperforms across all financial performance measures. In most cases, you would have better success owning AGF's stock rather than one of their funds. How is that for irony?

Revenue Growth: ★★★★★

Past five years: 45 percent

Pre-tax Income Growth: ★★★★★

Past five years: 47 percent

Total Return: ★★★★★

Past five years: 48 percent

Return on Capital Employed: ★★

Past five years: 10 percent

AGF Management Ltd. at a Glance

Fiscal year ended: November 1999

Revenue and net income in $ millions

	1995	1996	1997	1998	1999	4-Year Growth Average (%)	4-Year Growth Total (%)
Total Revenue	88	179	237	289	357	45.51	307.07
Net Income	17	22	40	49	62	40.08	265.23
Earnings/ Share ($)	0.54	0.617	1.01	1.19	1.52	30.88	181.48
Dividend/ Share ($)	0.25	0.2	0.17	0.26	0.3	8.33	20
Dividend Yield (%)	4.44	1.94	0.29	1.22	1.28	–	–
Price to Earnings (PE)	10.42	16.75	57.18	17.86	15.46	–	–

Stock Growth (High-Low-Close)

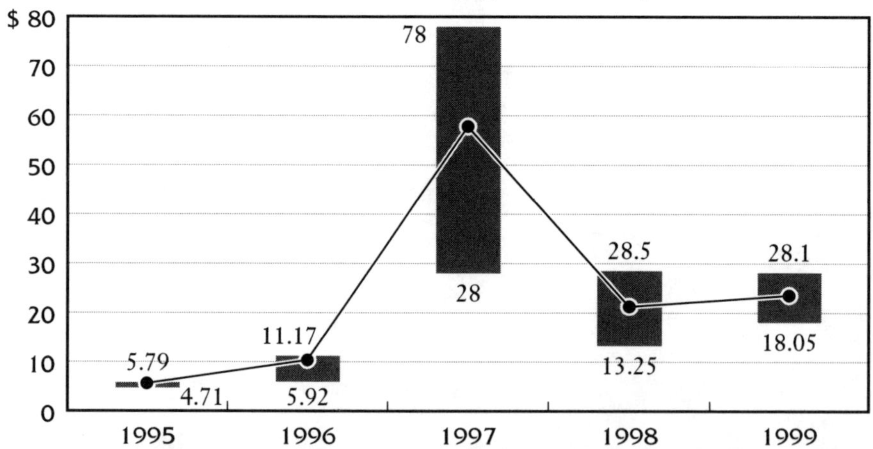

Close	5.62	10.33	57.75	21.25	23.5

17

CANADIAN NATIONAL RAILWAY CO.

935 de la Gauchetière West
Montreal, PQ H3B 2M9
(888) 888-5909
www.cn.ca

President, CEO: Paul M. Tellier

Revenue Growth	★★
Pre-tax Income Growth	★★★★★
Total Return	★★★★★
Return on Capital Employed	★★★★★
TSE: CNR	**17**

Canadian National Railway Co. is a railroad transportation company. It deals exclusively in freight transportation (as opposed to passenger service) and its business is divided into basic commodity groups: petroleum and chemicals, metals and minerals, forest products, coal, grain and fertilizers, intermodal (consumer products and manufactured goods, as well as shipping containers), and automotive (finished vehicles and parts).

For fiscal 1999 (year ending December 31, 1999) CN Rail reported revenue of $5.2 billion, versus $4.1 billion for fiscal 1998. By commodity group, fiscal 1999 revenue was grain and fertilizers, $1.1 billion; forest products, $995 million; petroleum and chemicals, $878 million; intermodal, $810 million; automotive, $483 million; coal, $402 million; metals and minerals, $398 million; and other items, $204 million.

During 1999 CN Rail merged with Illinois Central (through acquisition), which extended the company's reach south from Chicago to New Orleans. The merger created a "Y-shaped network" of approximately 27,000 kilometres of track in Canada and the United States, reaching from the Atlantic and Pacific oceans to the Gulf of Mexico. This rail network, in conjunction with a marketing deal with the Kansas City Southern Railway, is the first to link all three NAFTA partners.

In December 1999 CN Rail announced its intention to combine its business with that of the Texas-based Burlington Northern and Santa Fe Railway Company to create North American Railways Inc. The new company, to be in operation by mid-2001, would have revenue of over $18 billion per year, 60,000 employees, and approximately 80,000 kilometres of track. As of early 2000, however, the U.S. Service Transportation Board was in opposition to the proposal.

CN Rail employs approximately 23,500 people and is headquartered in Montreal.

The company's stock underwent a two-for-one split in September 1999.

CN Rail shares are traded on the Toronto and New York stock exchanges.

Revenue Growth: ★★

Past five years: 8 percent

Pre-tax Income Growth: ★★★★★

Past five years: 299 percent

Total Return: ★★★★★

Past five years: 25 percent

Return on Capital Employed: ★★★★★

Past five years: 113 percent

Canadian National Railway Co. at a Glance

Fiscal year ended: December 1999

Revenue and net income in $ millions

	1995	1996	1997	1998	1999	4-Year Growth Average (%)	4-Year Growth Total (%)
Total Revenue	3,954	3,995	4,313	4,101	5,261	8.09	33.06
Net Income	–1,085	850	403	109	602	126.27	155.48
Earnings/ Share ($)	–6.745	5.005	2.37	0.6	3.02	112.55	144.77
Dividend/ Share ($)	0	0.4	0.46	0.53	0.6	–	–
Dividend Yield (%)	0	1.54	1.37	1.33	1.57	–	–
Price to Earnings (PE)	N/A	5.2	14.2	66.46	12.65	–	–

Stock Growth (High-Low-Close)

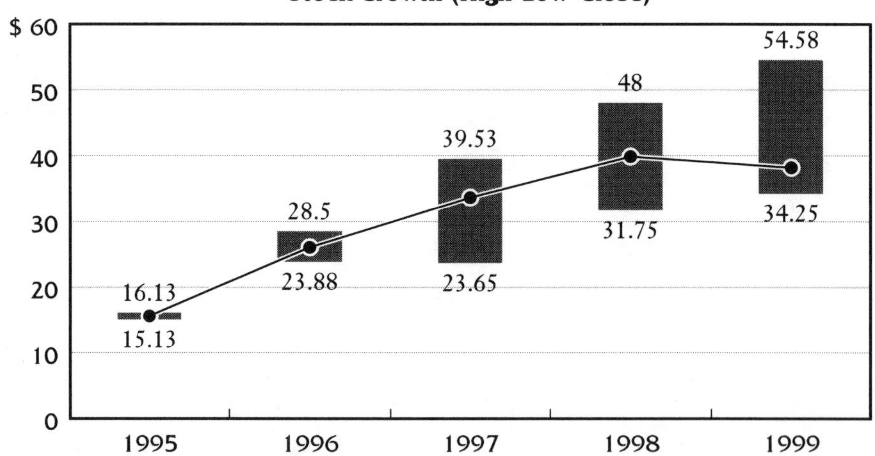

Close	15.63	26.05	33.65	39.88	38.2

18

SEARS CANADA INC.

222 Jarvis Street
Toronto, ON M5B 2B8
(416) 941-4425
www.sears.ca

Chairman, CEO: P.S. Walters
President, COO: J.R. Clifford

Revenue Growth	★★
Pre-tax Income Growth	★★★★★
Total Return	★★★★★
Return on Capital Employed	★★★★★
TSE: SCC	**17**

Sears Canada Inc. is the largest single general-merchandise and services retailer in Canada, with a chain of department stores and specialty stores across the country. The company has evolved from being the leader in catalogue shopping to the dominant department store force in Canada. As rivals Eaton's and The Bay have struggled and, in the case of Eaton's, gone bankrupt, Sears has excelled in remaking itself to respond to the challenges of U.S. competitors and e-tailing.

Ironically, the mastermind behind Sears, Paul Walters, was previously president of Zellers, the most profitable subsidiary of The Bay.

The company has 110 full-line stores, 25 furniture and appliance stores, 12 outlet stores, and 15 floor-covering stores. It also operates a travel business with 87 locations, and 67 auto centres.

For fiscal 1999 (year ending January 1, 2000) the company reported revenue of $6.1 billion, versus $5 billion in fiscal 1998, an increase of almost 22 percent.

Sears is making extensive efforts to promote its online retail presence, which began in 1996. In 1999 the company's catalogue operation was renamed Sears Online. Fiscal revenue derived from Internet sales was $22 million (a sevenfold increase versus fiscal 1998), representing approximately 150,000 orders.

Following the bankruptcy of the Eaton's department store chain, Sears purchased 16 Eaton's stores, including flagship stores in Toronto, Vancouver, Calgary, Ottawa, Winnipeg, and Victoria, as well as the Eaton's name and brands. An additional three Eaton's locations will be leased. The company plans to operate the flagship stores as upscale locations (due to open in fall 2000) under the Eaton's banner. The remainder will be converted to Sears stores.

The company's Sears card is the largest single-issue credit card in Canada.

Sears Canada is headquartered in Toronto and has almost 11,000 full-time employees and more than 35,000 part-time employees.

Revenue Growth: ★★

Past five years: 9 percent

Pre-tax Income Growth: ★★★★★

Past five years: 207 percent

Total Return: ★★★★★

Past five years: 41 percent

Return on Capital Employed: ★★★★★

Past five years: 33 percent

Sears Canada Inc. at a Glance

Fiscal year ended: December 1999

Revenue and net income in $ millions

						4-Year Growth	
	1995	1996	1997	1998	1999	Average (%)	Total (%)
Total Revenue	3,918	3,956	4,584	4,967	6,131	9.16	41.53
Net Income	12	9	117	146	200	314.5	1,536.07
Earnings/ Share ($)	0.13	0.09	1.1	1.38	1.86	287.92	1,330.77
Dividend/ Share ($)	0.24	0.24	0.24	0.24	0.24	–	0
Dividend Yield (%)	4	2.33	1.21	1.33	0.6	–	–
Price to Earnings (PE)	46.15	114.44	18	13.04	21.51	–	–

Stock Growth (High-Low-Close)

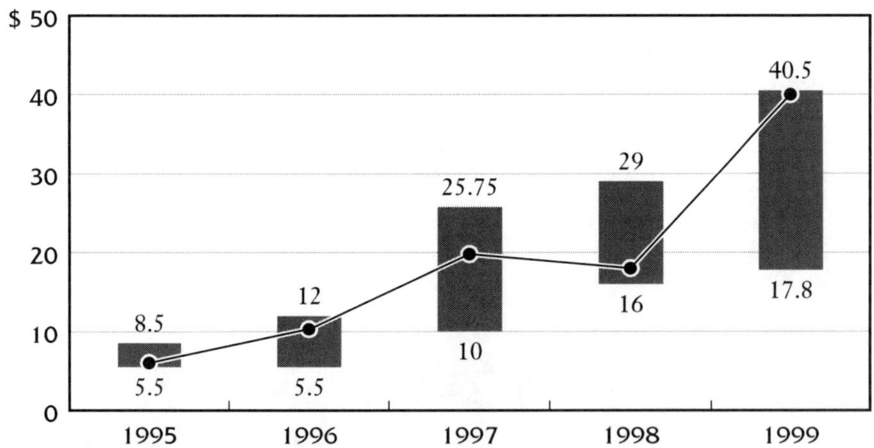

Close	6	10.3	19.8	18	40

19

PENN WEST PETROLEUM LTD.

111, 5th Avenue SW, Suite 800
Calgary, AB T2P 3Y6
(403) 777-2500

President: William E. Andrew

Revenue Growth	★★★★★
Pre-tax Income Growth	★★★★★
Total Return	★★★★★
Return on Capital Employed	★★
TSE: PWT	**17**

Calgary-based *Penn West Petroleum Ltd.* explores for, develops, and produces oil and natural gas in western Canada. The company has both working wells and a reserve of undeveloped land.

Despite a resurgence in the price of crude oil over the last year, companies such as Penn West have not seen a major reaction in their share price. This has been particularly true of companies with smaller market capitalizations, which includes Penn West. Nevertheless, despite the less than buoyant price of crude over the last five years, the company has stood out with a 28 percent compounded growth in earnings and a total return of over 44 percent. That kind of performance explains why Murray Edwards, one of Western Canada's better known merchant bankers, retains a major stake in the corporation (one of his other major holdings is Magellan Aerospace, featured in *The 50 Best Stocks to Own in Canada under $20*).

As of December 31, 1998, the company had over 2 million acres of gross undeveloped land ("gross" refers to all property in which the company has an interest), more than 1000 producing oil wells (gross), and more than 860 producing natural gas wells (gross).

In terms of daily production, as of September 30, 1999, the company reported 263 million cubic feet of natural gas and 23,700 barrels of crude oil and liquids.

Penn West had revenue of $184 million for fiscal 1998 (year ending December 31, 1998), versus $183 million in fiscal 1997. For the first nine months of fiscal 1999 the company reported revenue of $259 million, versus $147 million for the same period a year earlier, a 76 percent increase.

During fiscal 1998 the company drilled or participated in the drilling of over 150 new wells.

Penn West has been a part of the TSE 300 Composite Index since 1995.

Revenue Growth: ★★★★★

Past five years: 36 percent

Pre-tax Income Growth: ★★★★★

Past five years: 68 percent

Total Return: ★★★★★

Past five years: 41 percent

Return on Capital Employed: ★★

Past five years: 9 percent

Penn West Petroleum Ltd. at a Glance

Fiscal year ended: December 1999

Revenue and net income in $ millions

						4-Year Growth	
	1995	1996	1997	1998	1999	Average (%)	Total (%)
Total Revenue	112	144	183	184	344	35.8	206.96
Net Income	12	24	37	33	78	70.61	552.45
Earnings/ Share ($)	0.37	0.66	0.9	0.77	1.59	51.7	329.73
Dividend/ Share ($)	0	0	0	0	0	–	–
Dividend Yield (%)	0	0	0	0	0	–	–
Price to Earnings (PE)	18.58	21.21	17.17	21.43	17.77	–	–

Stock Growth (High-Low-Close)

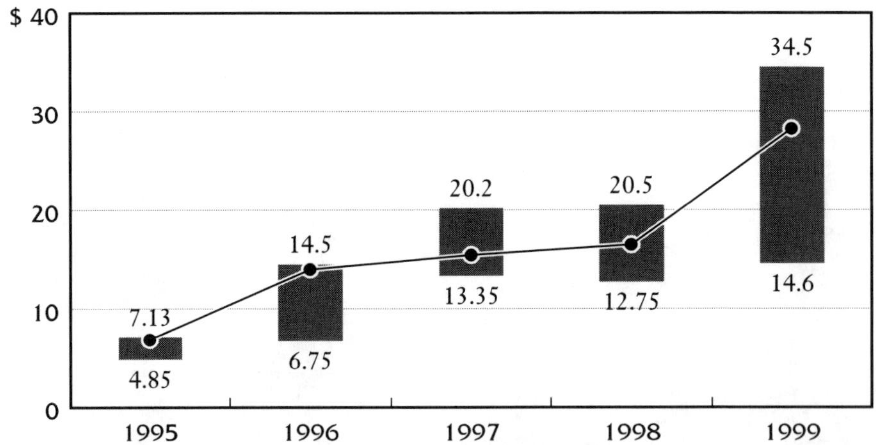

Close	6.88	14	15.45	16.5	28.25

20

ATS AUTOMATION TOOLING SYSTEMS INC.

250 Royal Oak Road, Box 32100
Cambridge, ON N3H 5M2
(519) 653-6500
www.atsautomation.com

President, CEO: K.D. Woerner

Revenue Growth	★★★★★
Pre-tax Income Growth	★★★★★
Total Return	★★★★★
Return on Capital Employed	★★
TSE: ATA	**17**

ATS Automation Tooling Systems Inc., based in Cambridge, Ontario, has been at the forefront of industrial automation for many years. It is gratifying that in ATS, Canada has a company that is considered without equal in the world. Customers like Intel and IBM rely on ATS's state-of-the-art machines to manufacture their most critical high-tech components.

ATS produces large-scale automated manufacturing and testing systems, as well as plastic and metal precision components for the automotive and electronics industries. The company employs roughly 2400 people in Canada, the United States, Europe, and Asia/Pacific.

The company has two major divisions: the Automated Systems Group and the Precision Components Group. The Automated Systems Group accounted for approximately 60 percent of the company's fiscal 1999 (year ending March 31, 1999) revenue of $515 million. According to the company, both groups derive the majority of their revenue from repeat customers (89 percent and 84 percent, respectively).

The Automated Systems Group designs, builds, and services automated manufacturing systems for the automotive, medical, electronics, computer, and packaging industries, among others. Approximately 63 percent of its fiscal 1999 revenue was derived from sales in the United States and Mexico, with Canada accounting for 17 percent, Europe for 15 percent, and Asia/Pacific for 5 percent. The average cost of an ATS system is approximately $2 million.

According to the company, ATS began fiscal 2000 with an automation systems backlog of $140 million, up 49 percent versus the previous year.

The Precision Components Group produces high-volume precision components and sub-assemblies for the automotive, electronics/ computer, and solar industries. It also offers such services as rapid prototyping, system design, and factory design and planning. Roughly 33 percent of this group's fiscal 1999 revenue came from sales in the Asia/Pacific region, with the United States and Mexico accounting for 31 percent, Europe for 23 percent, and Canada for 13 percent. In fiscal 1999 the company manufactured over 150 million units.

The company is making an effort to expand its business outside North America; on the whole, revenue generated outside North America increased by 800 percent from fiscal 1997 to fiscal 1999.

A microelectronics contract with a Fortune 500 company (ATS does not identify this company in any of its press releases) worth

$102 million in fiscal 1999 (roughly 50 percent of the Precision Components Group's revenue) will not generate significant revenue in fiscal 2000. Excluding this contract, however, this group's revenue grew 27 percent in fiscal 1999.

The company's common shares had two-for-one stock splits in December 1996 and December 1997. The company's share price took a nosedive in early 1999 following the announcement that some expected Intel orders were not going to materialize. The market incorrectly assumed that this meant that ATS's relationship with the world's number-one semiconductor manufacturer was somehow in peril, which it wasn't. Intel has subsequently awarded many large contracts to ATS and these fears have been dispelled.

The company remains a Canadian high-tech manufacturing success story.

Revenue Growth: ★★★★★

Past five years: 39 percent

Pre-tax Income Growth: ★★★★★

Past five years: 55 percent

Total Return: ★★★★★

Past five years: 55 percent

Return on Capital Employed: ★★

Past five years: 8 percent

ATS Automation Tooling Systems Inc. at a Glance

Fiscal year ended: March 2000

Revenue and net income in $ millions

	1995	1996	1997	1998	1999	4-Year Growth Average (%)	4-Year Growth Total (%)
Total Revenue	139	197	250	403	515	39.46	271.09
Net Income	8	19	20	27	37	56.99	384.6
Earnings/ Share ($)	0.18	0.41	0.37	0.5	0.65	45.79	261.11
Dividend/ Share ($)	0	0	0	0	0	–	–
Dividend Yield (%)	0	0	0	0	0	–	–
Price to Earnings (PE)	14.23	17.07	28.92	51	16.54	–	–

Stock Growth (High-Low-Close)

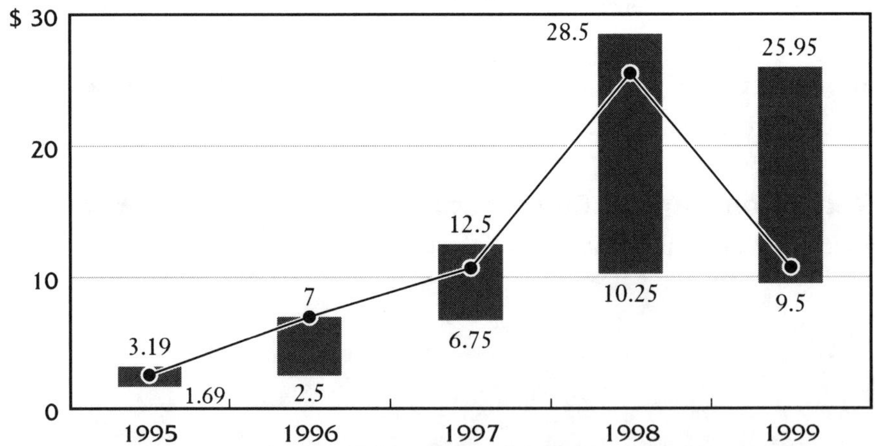

Close	2.56	7	10.7	25.5	10.75

21

MAGNA INTERNATIONAL INC.

337 Magna Drive
Aurora, ON L4G 7K1
(905) 726-2462
www.MagnaInt.com

Chairman: Frank Stronach
President, CEO: Donald Walker

Revenue Growth	★★★★★
Pre-tax Income Growth	★★★★★
Total Return	★
Return on Capital Employed	★★★★★
TSE: MG.A	**16**

One of the themes of business throughout the 1990s was "outsourcing." In their drive to focus on core competencies and cut costs corporations sought business partners that could perform various operations and services more efficiently than if they had been executed "in-house." Magna International exemplifies this type of company in the automotive sector. It not only produces parts and complete subsystems for the original equipment manufacturers (OEMs), but is now integral to the design and engineering processes as well.

Magna is a leading supplier of automotive interior and exterior body and chassis systems to every major auto manufacturer in North America and Europe, as well as a manufacturer of specialized vehicles.

Magna enjoys a sterling reputation in its industry, with *Forbes* magazine naming it the world's best automotive supplier in January 1999.

Magna has over 54,000 employees worldwide, located in North America, South America, Europe, and Asia. It has over 160 manufacturing operations and 29 product development and engineering centres.

Magna has made numerous acquisitions in its field over the last few years, most notably the award-winning Steyr-Daimler-Puch AG, which strengthened the company as a niche vehicle manufacturer.

The company reported nine-month results as of September 30, 1999, of $6.7 billion, a 29 percent increase over the same period in the previous year.

Magna began as the brainchild of founder Franck Stronach in a garage some 39 years ago. The company has recently been criticized for the grandiose visions of Stronach, who has stated his intention to take the company into areas that have nothing to do with producing bumpers for the next generation of minivans. Given the corporation's near-death experience in the early 1990s, investors are leery that Magna could once again stare into the abyss.

In March 2000, the company spun off its non-automotive assets into a separate company, called Magna Entertainment Corporation. This new company will invest in real estate, entertainment, and the gaming industry. The goal of the spinoff was to return Magna's focus to automotives, and it appears to have succeeded in achieving this.

Despite past concerns over the company's non-automotive forays, Magna remains one of Canada's premier industrial companies whose track record of revenue and earnings growth has been virtually uninterrupted.

Magna International's shares are listed on the Toronto, Montreal, and New York stock exchanges.

Revenue Growth: ★★★★★

Past five years: 45 percent

Pre-tax Income Growth: ★★★★★

Past five years: 53 percent

Total Return: ★

Past five years: 7 percent

Return on Capital Employed: ★★★★★

Past five years: 27 percent

Magna International Inc. at a Glance

Fiscal year ended: December 1999

Revenue and net income in US$ millions

	1995	1996	1997	1998	1999	4-Year Growth Average (%)	4-Year Growth Total (%)
Total Revenue	5,221	6,886	8,592	5,198	13,601	44.71	160.54
Net Income	285	537	472	210	625	54.68	119.13
Earnings/ Share ($)	4.203	6.949	5.822	2.372	6.903	45.22	64.24
Dividend/ Share ($)	0.969	1.014	1.202	0.337	1.613	82.46	66.46
Dividend Yield (%)	1.58	1.1	1.17	0.33	2.62	–	–
Price to Earnings (PE)	14.6	13.21	17.61	43.23	8.91	–	–

Stock Growth (High-Low-Close)

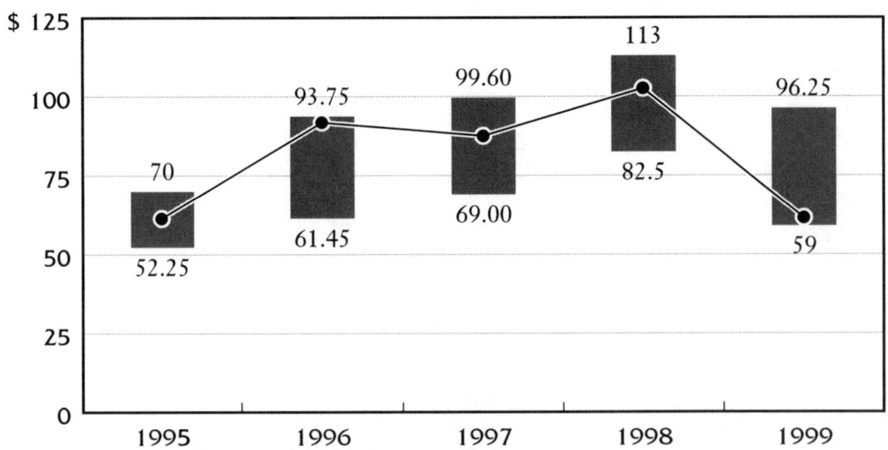

Close	61.35	91.80	87.50	102.55	61.50

22

CANADIAN PACIFIC LTD.

855, 2nd Street SW
Calgary, AB T2P 4Z5
(403) 218-8000
www.cp.ca

Chairman, President, CEO: D.P. O'Brien

Revenue Growth	★★★
Pre-tax Income Growth	★★★★★
Total Return	★★★
Return on Capital Employed	★★★★★
TSE: CP	**16**

This is a company that is often viewed by foreign capital markets as a proxy for Canada. Canadian Pacific Limited is the parent company of a number of subsidiaries, whose business is divided into three core areas: Transportation, Energy, and Hotels. Through these subsidiaries, the company has interests in Canada, the United States, Mexico, and Bermuda. The company had numerous other business interests that it spent most of the 1990s divesting, returning it to its original roots. Some have argued that this move has left the company less dynamic and more susceptible to economic cycles. We would argue, that generally speaking, companies that focus on their historical core competencies perform better over the long haul.

Revenue for Canadian Pacific for fiscal 1999 (year ending December 31, 1999) was $11.4 billion, versus $10.2 billion for fiscal 1998. For the first quarter of fiscal 2000 (ending March 31, 2000), the company reported revenue of $1.8 billion, versus $1.5 billion for the same period a year earlier.

In Transportation, the Canadian Pacific Railway Company (and its subsidiaries) provides freight transport over a rail network of approximately 22,000 kilometres in Canada and the northeastern and midwestern United States. CP Ships Holding Inc. (and its subsidiaries) provides container-shipping services in the North Atlantic, Latin America, and Australasia. In 1999, this segment accounted for 54 percent of total revenue.

In Energy, PanCanadian Petroleum Limited (86.6 percent owned by CP) is involved in crude-oil and natural gas exploration, development, production, and marketing, primarily in western Canada and off the coast of Nova Scotia, with international interests in Africa, Latin America, the UK, and Australia. Fording Inc. is a mining company with operations in Canada, the United States, and Mexico. In 1999, this segment accounted for 40 percent of total revenue.

In Hotels, Canadian Pacific Hotels & Resorts Inc. is the largest luxury and first-class hotel operator in North America, through its Delta Hotels and Fairmont Hotels & Resorts brands and affiliates. As of December 31, 1999, the company and its affiliates managed 69 properties in Canada, the United States, Mexico, Bermuda, and Barbados. In 1999, this segment accounted for 6 percent of total revenue.

While arguably no longer a true proxy for the Canadian economy, Canadian Pacific still has a well-earned position in most investment portfolios.

Based in Calgary, the company has approximately 42,000 employees worldwide.

Revenue Growth: ★★★

Past five years: 12 percent

Pre-tax Income Growth: ★★★★★

Past five years: 98 percent

Total Return: ★★★

Past five years: 11 percent

Return on Capital Employed: ★★★★★

Past five years: 1,337 percent

Canadian Pacific Ltd. at a Glance

Fiscal year ended: December 1999
Revenue and net income in US$ millions

						4-Year Growth	
	1995	1996	1997	1998	1999	Average (%)	Total (%)
Total Revenue	7,331	8,471	9,560	10,151	11,367	11.64	55.05
Net Income	–786	869	1,256	801	594	48.22	175.47
Earnings/ Share ($)	–2.3	2.52	3.64	2.39	1.76	48.33	176.52
Dividend/ Share ($)	0.36	0.48	0.48	0.54	0.56	12.38	55.56
Dividend Yield (%)	1.45	1.33	1.25	1.88	1.8	–	–
Price to Earnings (PE)	N/A	14.31	10.58	12.03	17.64	–	–

Stock Growth (High-Low-Close)

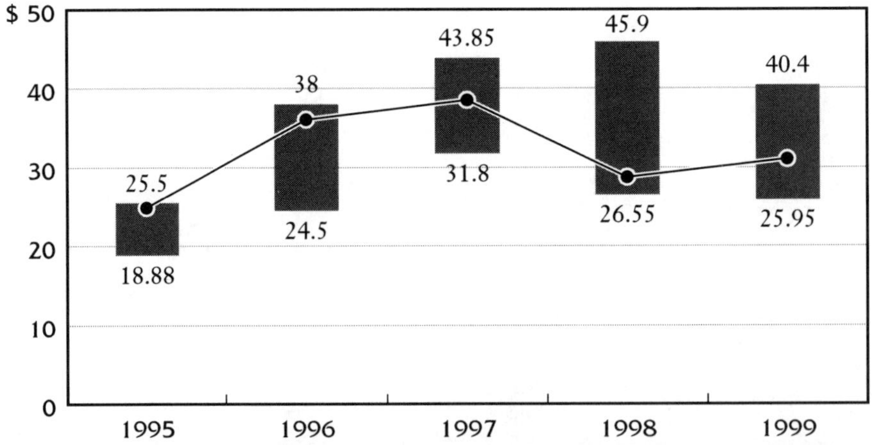

Close	24.88	36.05	38.5	28.75	31.05

23

THOMSON CORP.

Box 24, Toronto-Dominion Centre
Toronto, ON M5K 1A1
(416) 360-8700
www.thomcorp.com

Chairman: Kenneth R. Thomson
President, CEO: Richard J. Harrington

Revenue Growth	★★★★
Pre-tax Income Growth	★★★★★
Total Return	★★★★★
Return on Capital Employed	★
TSE: TOC	**15**

A lot of Canadians probably think of Thomson Corporation in terms of *The Globe and Mail*, the venerable daily newspaper. However, under Sir Kenneth's guidance, Thomson has morphed from a sleepy newspaper, travel, and retail empire into a leading new economy enterprise.

With the May 1998 sale of its leisure travel business interests, Thomson Corporation completed streamlining itself into what it calls an "information company." The company's vision is simply this: "We aspire to be the foremost information business in the world."

In addition to substantial newspaper publishing assets in North America (including *The Globe and Mail*), Thomson's businesses now include proprietary information products and services in the following areas:

- Reference, scientific, and health care
- Financial
- Legal and regulatory
- Learning

The company has chosen to target niche markets with specialized information and software-based solutions for clients in the above fields, particularly governments, private professionals, and academics. The bulk of the company's sales are in North America, although it holds assets in North America, the United Kingdom, Australia, and New Zealand.

As part of the overall strategy noted above, Thomson made 70 acquisitions in 1998 costing $830 million, and sold 30 non-core businesses for $410 million. Since 1993 the company has invested over $6 billion in acquisitions in pursuit of its goal.

With all of the focus on technology stocks vis-à-vis the Internet, investors should start to think of Thomson as an Internet player. As we saw with the AOL/Time Warner marriage in the United States, content is as important as the delivery medium. As an Internet content provider Thomson has the added advantage that a lot of its data/content is aimed at professional users who are generally willing to pay more than retail consumers. Unlike the dot-com start-ups, Thomson has revenue, earnings, and something very rare in the Internet world: a high barrier to entry. Thomson's information databases are proprietary and would be difficult and almost prohibitively expensive to duplicate.

Thomson Corporation is listed on the Toronto, Montreal, and London stock exchanges. Note that the Thomson family owns approximately 73 percent of the company's common shares.

Revenue Growth: ★★★★

Past five years: 16 percent

Pre-tax Income Growth: ★★★★★

Past five years: 28 percent

Total Return: ★★★★★

Past five years: 24 percent

Return on Capital Employed: ★

Past five years: 5 percent

Thomson Corp. at a Glance

Fiscal year ended: December 1999

Revenue and net income in US$ millions

	1995	1996	1997	1998	1999	4-Year Growth Average (%)	4-Year Growth Total (%)
Total Revenue	6,618	7,193	8,367	9,595	8,359	16.31	80.61
Net Income	1,090	796	828	2,825	814	36.74	–25.35
Earnings/ Share ($)	1.828	1.302	1.302	4.546	1.25	36.97	–31.62
Dividend/ Share ($)	0.7	0.765	0.844	0.96	0.956	8.24	36.57
Dividend Yield (%)	3.68	2.53	2.15	2.67	2.52	–	–
Price to Earnings (PE)	10.39	23.23	30.15	7.9	30.4	–	–

Stock Growth (High-Low-Close)

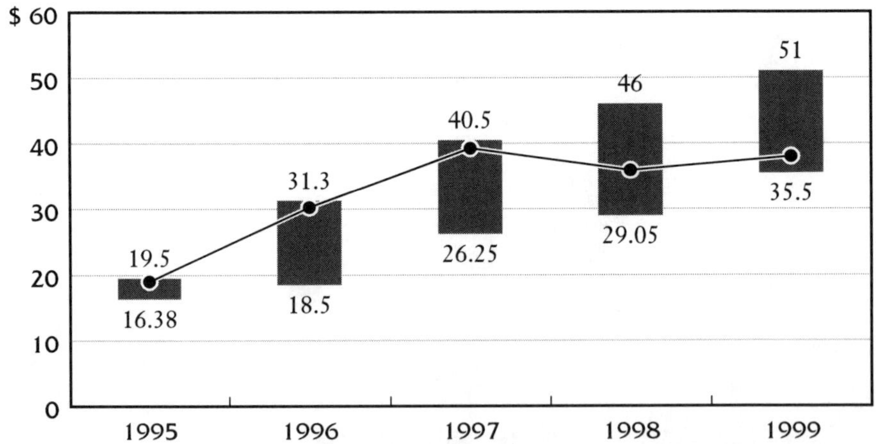

Close	19	30.25	39.25	35.9	38

24

C-MAC INDUSTRIES INC.

1010 Sherbrooke West, Suite 1610
Montreal, PQ H3A 2R7
(514) 282-7629
www.cmac.ca

President, Chairman, CEO: Dennis Wood

Revenue Growth	★★★★★
Pre-tax Income Growth	★★★★★
Total Return	★★★★★
Return on Capital Employed	0
TSE: CMS	**15**

C-MAC is a Montreal-based company that designs and manufactures advanced electronic systems and components. The company also provides assembly services on contract for the instrumentation, telecommunications, automotive, defence, and aerospace industries. The company employs over 4100 workers in Canada, the United States, Europe, India, and China. With the increasing trend towards outsourcing, companies like C-MAC and its brethren have enjoyed steady organic growth.

C-MAC has two main product divisions: the Electronic Systems Division and the Microtechnology Division. The Electronic Systems Division produces complete network systems, packaging systems, manufacturing services (such as product design, packaging, and shipping), precision sheet-metal fabrication, printed circuit boards, and interconnect products (such as frames, cabinets, and backpanels). The Microtechnology Division manufactures microcircuits and quartz-crystal frequency devices.

The company also manufactures energy management products and systems.

In fiscal 1998 (year ending December 31, 1998) the Electronic Systems Division accounted for 62 percent, and the Microtechnology Division for 37 percent, of revenue totalling $646 million (versus $414 million in the previous year, a 56 percent increase).

In the nine-month period ending October 2, 1999, the company earned $782 million, versus $420 million for the same period in the previous year.

During 1999 C-MAC made several notable acquisitions. In September it purchased Montreal-based electromechanical systems company LG Technologies Group Inc., and in October it acquired UK-based Blue Star Engineering, a manufacturer of metal enclosures and accessories. C-MAC also purchased several assets from Nortel Networks relating to electromechanical sub-assembly design and manufacture.

The company reported an order book of deliverables at the end of fiscal 1998 totalling $315 million, 58 percent higher than in the previous year.

C-MAC is listed on the Montreal and Toronto stock exchanges.

Revenue Growth: ★★★★★

Past five years: 47 percent

Pre-tax Income Growth: ★★★★★

Past five years: 56 percent

Total Return: ★★★★★

Past five years: 102 percent

Return on Capital Employed: 0

Past five years: 2 percent

C-MAC Industries Inc. at a Glance

Fiscal year ended: December 1999

Revenue and net income in $ millions

	1995	1996	1997	1998	1999	4-Year Growth Average (%)	4-Year Growth Total (%)
Total Revenue	265	318	414	646	1,175	46.96	342.48
Net Income	10	15	20	25	45	46.25	342.52
Earnings/ Share ($)	0.195	0.285	0.395	0.49	0.76	40.98	289.74
Dividend/ Share ($)	0	0	0	0	0	–	–
Dividend Yield (%)	0	0	0	0	0	–	–
Price to Earnings (PE)	10.64	17.02	22.91	25.77	54.28	–	–

Stock Growth (High-Low-Close)

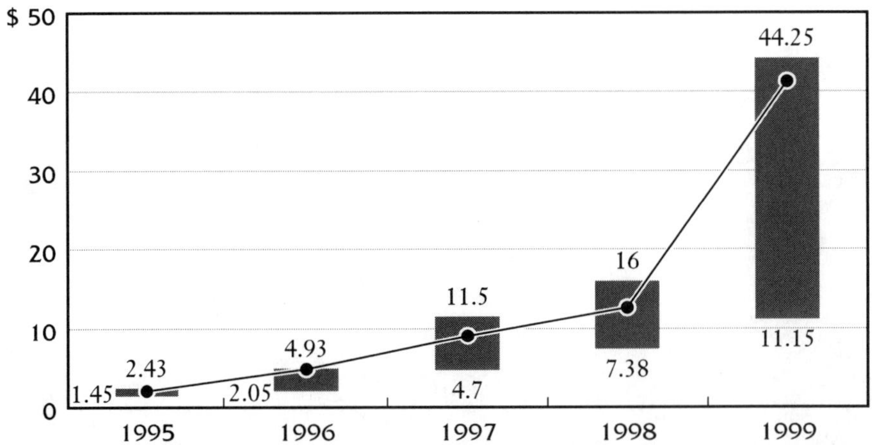

	1995	1996	1997	1998	1999
Close	2.08	4.85	9.05	12.63	41.25

25

EMPIRE COMPANY LTD.

115 King Street
Stellarton, NS B0K 1S0
(902) 755-4440
www.empireco.ca

President, Director, CEO: Paul D. Sobey

Revenue Growth	★★★★★
Pre-tax Income Growth	★★★★★
Total Return	★★★★★
Return on Capital Employed	–★
TSE: EMP.A	**14**

Who says they only catch fish on the east coast? Nova Scotia–based *Empire Company Ltd.* is a diversified company with three major business divisions: Food Distribution, Real Estate, and Investment.

The Food Distribution division, Sobeys Inc., went public in 1998 on the Toronto and Montreal stock exchanges. Empire owns approximately 62 percent of Sobeys, which operates almost 1400 stores across Canada. Store banners include Sobeys, IGA, Foodland, and Price Chopper. Sobeys Inc. is the second-largest food distributor in Canada.

The revenue derived from Sobeys Inc. is by far the company's largest component, accounting for $6.2 billion of Empire's $6.4 billion total revenue for fiscal 1999 (year ending April 30, 1999). This represents a 97.5 percent increase in revenue versus the previous year. This large growth is due to the $1.5 billion acquisition of the assets of The Oshawa Group, which tripled the size of Sobeys' food operations.

For the six-month period ending October 31, 1999, the Food Distribution group generated $5.5 billion in revenues.

Empire's Real Estate division consists of substantial property in Atlantic Canada that is under the control of two wholly owned subsidiaries: Atlantic Shopping Centres Ltd. and Sobey Leased Properties Ltd. Atlantic Shopping Centres, as the name suggests, controls enclosed shopping centre properties, while Sobey Leased Properties controls free-standing stores and shopping plazas, largely in support of the company's food retailing business. Overall, the two companies had over 11 million square feet of commercial property under management at the end of fiscal 1999.

Fiscal 1999 revenue for the Real Estate division was $148 million, versus $139 million in fiscal 1998. For the six-month period ending October 31, 1999, the division accounted for revenue of $52 million.

The company's Investment division consists of investments in U.S. food retailing and in Wajax Limited, a Canadian distribution company, of which Empire owns 48 percent. Empire also owns Empire Theatres, Atlantic Canada's largest movie exhibitor, with over 100 screens at 20 locations.

Fiscal 1999 revenue for the Investment division was $38 million, versus $64 million in the previous year. It should be noted that during fiscal 1999 Empire sold the majority of its liquid investment holdings for approximately $160 million, largely to fund the Oshawa Group acquisition.

For the first six months of fiscal 2000 (ending October 31, 1999) Empire derived $24 million in revenue from its Investment division.

While Empire Company is usually thought of in terms of its Sobeys stores, the broad diversification of the corporation's assets and their relatively "recession-proof" characteristics make this a logical choice for defensive investors. With the company's aggressive expansion westward into Ontario and the home turf of Loblaws stores, Empire has clearly signalled its intention to become a dominant force across the country.

Revenue Growth: ★★★★★
Past five years: 28 percent

Pre-tax Income Growth: ★★★★★
Past five years: 26 percent

Total Return: ★★★★★
Past five years: 23 percent

Return on Capital Employed: –★
Past five years: –1 percent

Empire Company Ltd. at a Glance

Fiscal year ended: April 2000

Revenue and net income in $ millions

	1995	1996	1997	1998	1999	4-Year Growth Average (%)	4-Year Growth Total (%)
Total Revenue	2,700	2,915	3,150	3,320	6,378	28.38	136.25
Net Income	41	22	53	88	135	54.1	227.87
Earnings/ Share ($)	0.93	0.41	1.33	2.31	3.53	73.74	279.57
Dividend/ Share ($)	0.2	0.215	0.22	0.242	0.273	8.16	36.5
Dividend Yield (%)	1.5	1.75	1.4	0.89	1.05	–	–
Price to Earnings (PE)	14.38	30	11.8	11.8	7.37	–	–

Stock Growth (High-Low-Close)

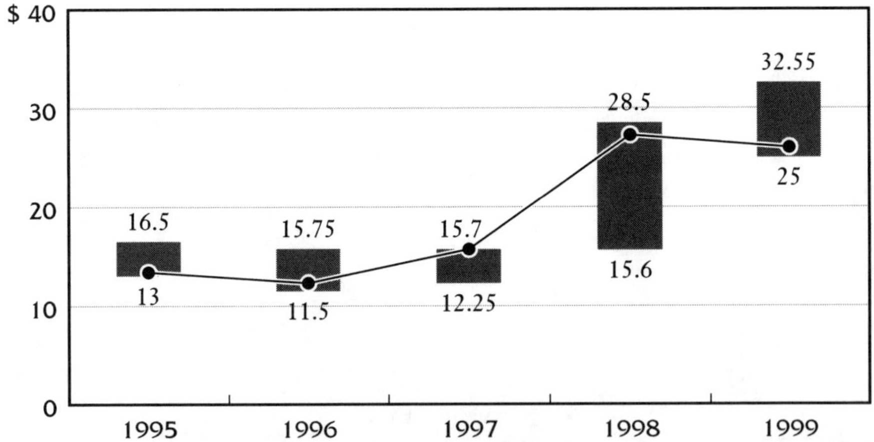

Close	13.38	12.3	15.7	27.25	26

26

A.L. VAN HOUTTE LIMITÉE

8300, 19th Avenue
Montreal, PQ H1Z 4J8
(514) 593-7711
www.alvanhoutte.com

President, CEO: Paul-André Guillotte

Revenue Growth	★★★★
Pre-tax Income Growth	★★★★★
Total Return	★★★★★
Return on Capital Employed	0
TSE: VH	**14**

A.L. Van Houtte Limitée is a gourmet-coffee company. The company's business is divided into two principal business groups: Coffee Service and Manufacture of Equipment, and Roasting and Marketing of Gourmet Coffee.

The Service and Equipment group is responsible for coffee service (the provision of coffee in institutional settings, such as offices, hospitals, and industrial plants) and the design and manufacture of the company's single-cup brewing equipment used by the coffee service operations. Van Houtte, through its subsidiaries, is North America's largest designer, manufacturer, marketer, and distributor of single-cup brewing equipment. The company provides coffee service across Canada and in 27 U.S. states.

The Roasting and Marketing group is the leading gourmet-coffee roaster in Canada, roasting and packaging a wide variety of coffee beans and ground coffee. These products are marketed across Canada through retail food stores and restaurants, hotels, and other food-service outlets.

The Roasting and Marketing group is also responsible for the largest network of café-bistros in Quebec (73 franchise and corporate outlets).

For fiscal 1999 (year ending April 3, 1999) the company reported revenue of $235 million, versus $207 million in fiscal 1998. The Service and Equipment group was responsible for almost 72 percent of fiscal 1999 revenue, with the Roasting and Marketing group accounting for the rest. Geographically, Quebec accounted for 35 percent of fiscal 1999 revenue, followed by western Canada (28 percent), the United States (17 percent), Ontario (16 percent), the Atlantic provinces (3 percent), and exports (1 percent).

For the first 40 weeks of fiscal 2000 (ending January 8, 2000) the company reported revenue of $189 million, versus $175 million for the same period one year earlier.

Van Houtte is headquartered in Montreal and employs approximately 1400 people.

Van Houtte is listed on the Montreal and Toronto stock exchanges, and has been included in the TSE 300 since 1998.

Revenue Growth: ★★★★

Past five years: 16 percent

Pre-tax Income Growth: ★★★★★

Past five years: 24 percent

Total Return: ★★★★★

Past five years: 25 percent

Return on Capital Employed: 0

Past five years: 3 percent

A.L. Van Houtte Limitée at a Glance

Fiscal year ended: March 2000

Revenue and net income in $ millions

	1995	1996	1997	1998	1999	4-Year Growth Average (%)	4-Year Growth Total (%)
Total Revenue	131	164	171	207	235	15.86	78.43
Net Income	7	9	10	14	17	26.5	155.09
Earnings/ Share ($)	0.39	0.46	0.54	0.68	0.79	19.36	102.56
Dividend/ Share ($)	0.075	0.08	0.085	0.1	0.14	17.64	86.67
Dividend Yield (%)	1.02	0.86	0.62	0.33	0.49	–	–
Price to Earnings (PE)	18.91	20.24	25.46	44.12	36.08	–	–

Stock Growth (High-Low-Close)

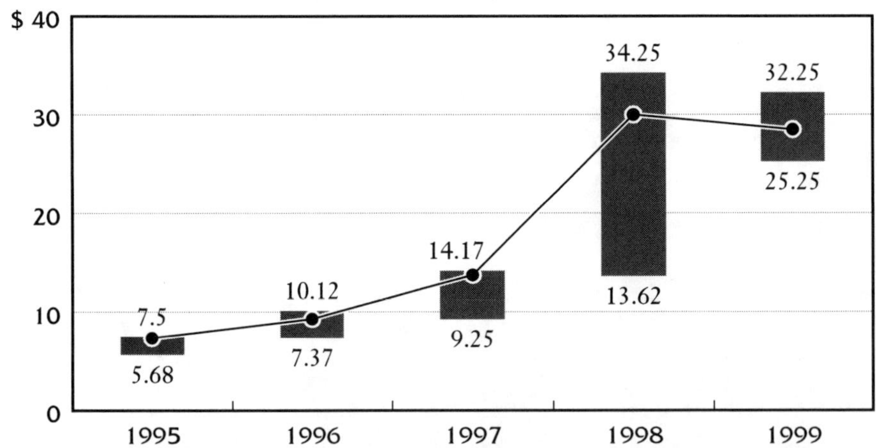

Close	7.38	9.31	13.75	30	28.5

27

LOBLAW COMPANIES LTD.

22 St. Clair Avenue East
Toronto, ON M4T 2S8
(416) 922-8500
www.loblaw.com

Chairman: W. Galen Weston
President: Richard J. Currie

Revenue Growth	★★★★
Pre-tax Income Growth	★★★★★
Total Return	★★★★★
Return on Capital Employed	0
TSE: L	**14**

Loblaw Companies offers one of the ultimate recession-proof stocks that also happens to be a growth stock. Its stores span the U.S. and Canada. We all have to eat and that ensures that grocers make money in good times and in bad. Most grocers are saddled with narrow profit margins, high variability in their costs, and stagnant growth, but not Loblaw. While its revenue growth has been modest, its income growth and shareholder returns have outpaced the bulk of the companies on the TSE for the last five years.

Loblaw Companies is Canada's largest food distributor, with over 1110 stores and 113,000 employees. Store banners include Loblaws, Zehrs, Maxi, Provigo, and IGA (in Atlantic Canada), among many others.

Over the last few years Loblaw Companies has engaged in a strategy of increasing the size of its stores, through the construction of new, large-format, corporate-owned and franchised stores as well as the refurbishment of selected existing stores.

The company made two major acquisitions at the end of 1998: Provigo (for $1.7 billion), which operates stores in Ontario and Quebec, and Agora Foods (for $81 million), which operates stores in Atlantic Canada.

The company has recently expanded into the banking business with President's Choice Financial, offering a variety of personal, in-store banking services.

One of Loblaw Companies' most significant strengths is its controlled-label program. The company's no-name, President's Choice, and Club Pack brand products had sales of almost $2 billion in 1998.

As of early 1999 the company reported that it had almost 225 in-store pharmacies. The company also noted that it was Canada's largest film developer.

Note that approximately 63 percent of Loblaw Companies was owned by George Weston Ltd. (GWL) as of March 1999. GWL is a holding company with two principal business segments: Loblaw Companies Limited and Weston Food Processing, which consists of a range of bakery, dairy, and fish processing operations.

While many view Loblaw Companies as a defensive stock by virtue of the necessity of human nourishment, its innovative marketing, store designs, and private and brand label strategies make it a great choice for growth investors.

Revenue Growth: ★★★★

Past five years: 19 percent

Pre-tax Income Growth: ★★★★★

Past five years: 27 percent

Total Return: ★★★★★

Past five years: 39 percent

Return on Capital Employed: 0

Past five years: 2 percent

Loblaw Companies Ltd. at a Glance

Fiscal year ended: December 1999

Revenue and net income in $ millions

	1995	1996	1997	1998	1999	4-Year Growth Average (%)	4-Year Growth Total (%)
Total Revenue	9,854	9,848	11,008	12,497	18,783	18.89	90.61
Net Income	147	174	213	261	376	26.84	155.78
Earnings/ Share ($)	0.6	0.72	0.88	1.06	1.37	22.98	128.33
Dividend/ Share ($)	0.11	0.12	0.15	0.2	0.22	19.36	100
Dividend Yield (%)	1.07	0.84	0.58	0.53	0.62	–	–
Price to Earnings (PE)	17.15	19.79	29.55	35.28	25.73	–	–

Stock Growth (High-Low-Close)

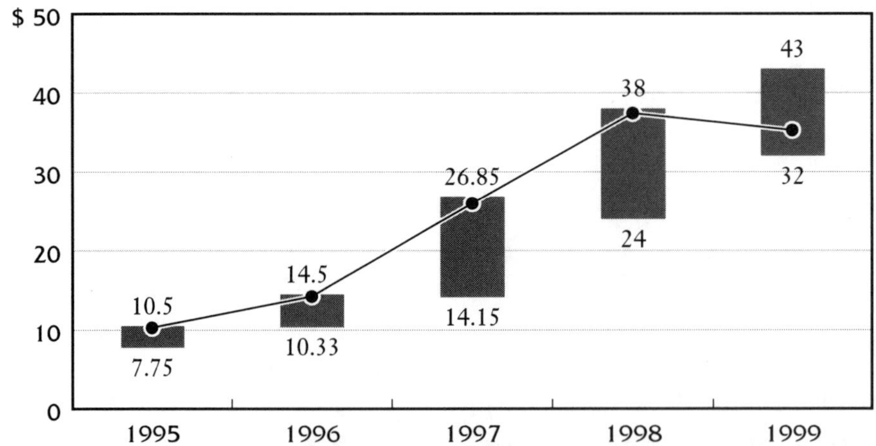

Close	10.29	14.25	26	37.4	35.25

28

ENSIGN RESOURCE SERVICE GROUP INC.

400, 5th Avenue SW, Suite 900
Calgary, AB T2P 0L6
(403) 262-1361
www.ensigngroup.com

President: Selby Porter

Revenue Growth	★★★★★
Pre-tax Income Growth	★★★★★
Total Return	★★★★★
Return on Capital Employed	–★
TSE: ESI	**14**

Headquartered in Calgary, Ensign Resource Service Group is an oil field contractor with eight divisions: four that provide oil and natural gas drilling services in western Canada and the Rocky Mountain region of the United States, three that provide oil and natural gas well servicing in western Canada, and one that provides manufacturing and production services to the Canadian oil and natural gas industries. The advantage of investing in a company such as Ensign is that it is one of the best proxies for exposure to oil prices. While oil and gas companies obviously fulfil this role as well, oil field services companies do not bear the exploration risks that producers do: they are paid whether the hole is dry or not.

For fiscal 1998 (year ending December 31, 1998) Ensign reported revenue of $419 million (77 percent from Canada, 23 percent from the United States), versus $517 million for fiscal 1997. This drop reflects a decline in the utilization rates of the company's rig fleet. In fiscal 1998 the utilization rate in Canada of the company's drilling rigs was 39.8 percent, versus 72.3 percent in the previous year. In the United States the utilization rate was 37.6 percent, versus 52.2 percent. As for the company's well-servicing rigs, the utilization rate was 45.4 percent, versus 92.9 percent.

For the nine-month period ending September 30, 1999, the company had sales of $242 million, versus $336 million in the same nine-month period in the previous year.

The company's rig fleet increased in fiscal 1998 to 182 drilling rigs (136 in Canada, 46 in the United States) and 115 well-servicing rigs, from 149 and 95, respectively, in fiscal 1997. These increases reflect Ensign's mid-1998 acquisition of Artisan Corporation. As of September 30, 1999, the company's fleet had further increased, with an additional 2 drilling rigs and 11 well-servicing rigs in Canada.

As of the end of fiscal 1998 Ensign Group was the third-largest land-based oil and natural gas drilling contractor in North America, and the third-largest well-servicing contractor in Canada.

One of the beauties of owning Ensign versus an oil and gas exploration/producer company is that, as stated above, Ensign makes money whether a hole hits the motherlode or comes up dry. The major driver for Ensign is the price of oil, as it is for most energy-based companies. The difference lies in the company's ability to reign in costs during periods of depressed pricing, unlike the producers who are forced to sit on large unproductive assets, sometimes for years.

Because of the recent volatility in the price of oil, investors interested in Ensign or companies like it should pay close attention to the corresponding volatility in the prices of these stocks.

Ensign Resource Service Group employs 3750 people.

Revenue Growth: ★★★★★

Past five years: 29 percent

Pre-tax Income Growth: ★★★★★

Past five years: 37 percent

Total Return: ★★★★★

Past five years: 61 percent

Return on Capital Employed: –★

Past five years: –2 percent

Ensign Resource Service Group Inc. at a Glance

Fiscal year ended: December 1999

Revenue and net income in $ millions

	1995	1996	1997	1998	1999	4-Year Growth Average (%)	4-Year Growth Total (%)
Total Revenue	181	245	517	419	372	29.13	106.08
Net Income	17	26	68	49	30	36.73	74
Earnings/ Share ($)	0.87	1.26	3.25	2.12	1.23	31.5	41.38
Dividend/ Share ($)	0.1	0.2	0.24	0.445	0.463	52.6	363
Dividend Yield (%)	1.43	0.79	0.69	3.3	1.38	–	–
Price to Earnings (PE)	8.05	20.04	10.65	6.37	27.24	–	–

Stock Growth (High-Low-Close)

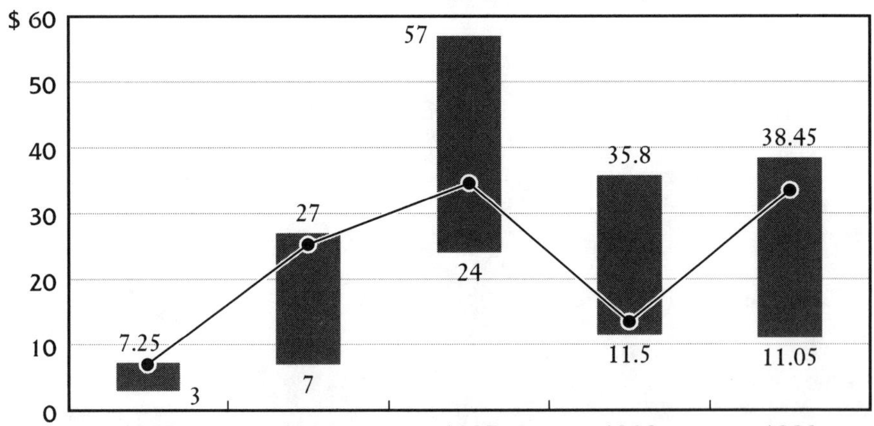

Close	7	25.25	34.6	13.5	33.5

29

MOFFAT COMMUNICATIONS LTD.

CKY Building, Polo Park, P.O. Box 220, Station "L"
Winnipeg, MB R3G 0L7
(204) 788-3440
www.moffat.ca

President, Chairman: Randall L. Moffat

Revenue Growth	★★★★★
Pre-tax Income Growth	★★★★★
Total Return	★★★★★
Return on Capital Employed	–★
TSE: MOF	**14**

Moffat Communications Ltd. operates cable-television assets in Canada and the United States, as well as television assets in Canada. The company also offers high-speed Internet access and related services.

Through a wholly owned subsidiary, Videon CableSystems Inc., the company operates cable systems in Manitoba, Alberta, and northern Ontario. Another subsidiary, Moffat International Corp., serves cable and Internet subscribers in Texas and Florida. The company also owns CKY-TV, a CTV Network affiliate in Manitoba, and 77 percent of

Lifestyle Television (1994) Ltd., otherwise known as the Women's Television Network specialty cable channel.

The company reported fiscal 1999 revenue (year ending August 31, 1999) of $233 million (versus $141 million in fiscal 1998), with the Canadian cable and Internet service segment accounting for 61 percent, U.S. cable and Internet accounting for 20 percent, and Canadian television accounting for 19 percent. The company attributes the large revenue increase in fiscal 1999 to the acquisition of 25 cable systems in Alberta during 1998.

Other 1999 highlights include a 33 percent boost in the common share dividend payable for the seventh year in a row from $0.09 per share to $0.12 per share. This, along with an impressive 142 percent total return in 1999 (stock price appreciation plus dividend yield) and a total return of over 60 percent over the last five years, is a good example of why Moffat is on our list.

For the first three months of fiscal 2000 the company reported revenue of $63 million, versus $58 million for the same period one year earlier.

As of August 31, 1999, the company reported over 320,000 cable subscribers in Canada and more than 60,000 in the United States. The company also reported almost 10,000 high-speed Internet customers in Canada, and over 1000 in the United States.

Moffat's stock split on a two-for-one basis in April 1999.

Moffat is based in Winnipeg and employs approximately 770 people.

Revenue Growth: ★ ★ ★ ★ ★

Past five years: 28 percent

Pre-tax Income Growth: ★ ★ ★ ★ ★

Past five years: 26 percent

Total Return: ★ ★ ★ ★ ★

Past five years: 58 percent

Return on Capital Employed: –★

Past five years: –1 percent

Moffat Communications Ltd. at a Glance

Fiscal year ended: August 1999

Revenue and net income in $ millions

	1995	1996	1997	1998	1999	4-Year Growth Average (%)	4-Year Growth Total (%)
Total Revenue	92	106	118	141	233	27.89	153.49
Net Income	9	11	14	25	21	26.05	124.23
Earnings/ Share ($)	0.242	0.295	0.37	0.63	0.54	25.83	123.14
Dividend/ Share ($)	0.05	0.06	0.07	0.09	0.12	24.64	140
Dividend Yield (%)	1.48	1.24	1.08	1.01	0.56	–	–
Price to Earnings (PE)	13.95	16.44	17.57	14.09	39.81	–	–

Stock Growth (High-Low-Close)

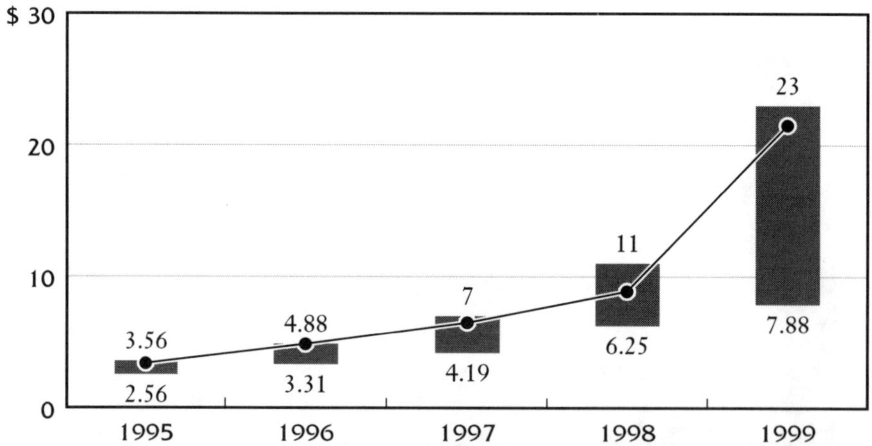

	1995	1996	1997	1998	1999
Close	3.38	4.85	6.5	8.88	21.5

30

LINAMAR CORP.

301 Massey Road
Guelph, ON N1K 1B2
(519) 836-7550
www.linamar.ca

Chairman, CEO: F. Hasenfratz

Revenue Growth	★ ★ ★ ★ ★
Pre-tax Income Growth	★ ★ ★ ★ ★
Total Return	★ ★ ★ ★
Return on Capital Employed	–★
TSE: LNR	**13**

Linamar Corp. manufactures precision-machined components, assemblies, and castings. Its primary market is the automotive industry, which accounted for approximately 86 percent of the company's sales of $1.3 billion in fiscal 1999 (year ending December 31, 1999).

Although smaller than Magna International Inc., another company featured in this book, Linamar shares a similar history in the sense that it was founded by a European émigré and has had a long and steady record of growth. Linamar has never deviated from its core business as Magna did with forays into publishing and entertainment concerns. As such, Linamar's shareholders have not had to endure the volatility and "near death" experience that has intermittently beset Magna over the last ten years.

Linamar has also escaped the liquidity difficulties many rapidly growing manufacturing companies face. The company's judicious use of debt has ensured that its ability to withstand the economy's ups and down has rarely been encumbered. While the company's stock price does ebb and flow with the fortunes of the automotive industry, Linamar's balance sheet and management track record have made it a consistent relative outperformer.

The company controls almost 30 facilities worldwide, in Canada (Ontario), the United States (Michigan and Kentucky), Mexico, and Hungary.

As noted, fiscal 1999 sales were $1.3 billion, versus $1 billion in fiscal 1998. Sales by geographical segment for fiscal 1999 were $1.1 billion from Canada, $59 million from the United States, $46 million from Mexico, and $37 million from Hungary.

In a joint venture with Wescast Industries Inc., an iron exhaust manifold manufacturer for the truck industry, Linamar plans to build an iron exhaust manifold design and production facility in western Hungary by 2001.

Linamar is headquartered in Guelph, Ontario, and employs approximately 8400 people worldwide.

Revenue Growth: ★★★★★
Past five years: 23 percent

Pre-tax Income Growth: ★★★★★
Past five years: 24 percent

Total Return: ★★★★
Past five years: 19 percent

Return on Capital Employed: –★
Past five years: –2 percent

Linamar Corp. at a Glance

Fiscal year ended: December 1999

Revenue and net income in $ millions

	1995	1996	1997	1998	1999	4-Year Growth Average (%)	4-Year Growth Total (%)
Total Revenue	546	608	771	998	1,252	23.28	129.43
Net Income	38	62	108	84	66	23.93	74.92
Earnings/ Share ($)	0.547	0.873	1.51	1.17	0.92	22.17	68.19
Dividend/ Share ($)	0.093	0.107	0.133	0.133	0.16	14.91	72.04
Dividend Yield (%)	1.21	0.73	0.48	0.51	1.16	–	–
Price to Earnings (PE)	14.02	16.8	18.32	22.22	14.95	–	–

Stock Growth (High-Low-Close)

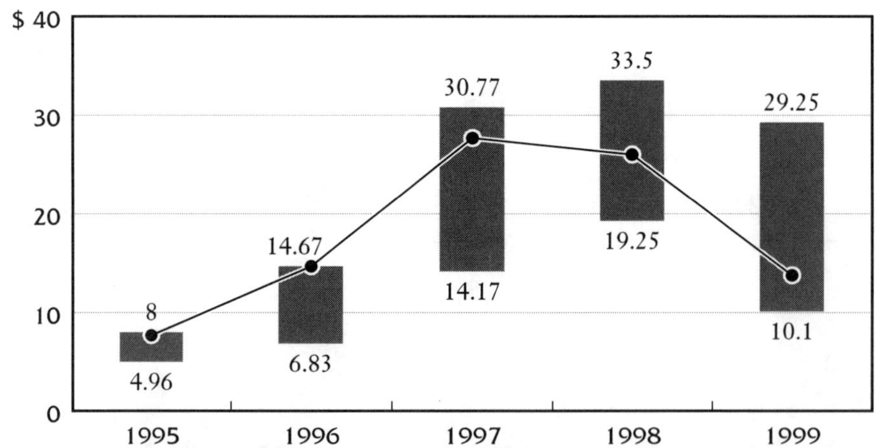

Close	7.67	14.67	27.67	26	13.75

31

JEAN COUTU GROUP (PJC) INC.

530 Beriault Street
Longueuil, PQ J4G 1S8
(450) 646-9760
www.jeancoutu.com

Chairman, CEO: Jean Coutu
President, COO: François Jean Coutu

Revenue Growth	★★★★
Pre-tax Income Growth	★★★★
Total Return	★★★★★
Return on Capital Employed	0
TSE: PJC.A	**13**

Though not as well known outside of Quebec, this company is an example of how it is possible for retailers to compete successfully with U.S.-based category killers like Wal-Mart. Jean Coutu Group is a pharmaceutical and para-pharmaceutical product distributor and retailer with operations in both Canada and the United States. The company operates over 250 franchised pharmacy "establishments" in Canada, mostly in Quebec, as well as in Ontario and New Brunswick, making it the second-largest pharmaceutical retail network in the country. Through its wholly owned subsidiary, Jean Coutu Group (PJC) U.S.A. Inc., the company also owns over 250 pharmacies in the northeastern United States under the Brooks Pharmacy banner.

The company's Canadian establishment model is designed so that each outlet has a pharmaceutical section, a photo counter, a cosmetics counter, and a commercial section for the sale of household goods and other consumer products. According to the company, it is the largest photo developer in Quebec.

In fiscal 1999 (year ending May 31, 1999) the company reported revenue of $2.3 billion, of which Canadian operations accounted for $1.1 billion and U.S. operations accounted for $1.2 billion. Figures for fiscal 1998 were $1.9 billion, $1 billion, and $900 million, respectively.

For the six-month period ending November 30, 1999, the company reported revenue of $1.3 billion (versus $1.1 billion for the same period one year earlier): $611 million from Canada and $639 million from the United States.

During fiscal 1999 the company acquired 5 independent U.S. pharmacies and City Drug Inc., which has 11 outlets in Vermont and New York.

The company is based in Montreal and has approximately 900 corporate employees; it employs approximately 11,000 people in Canada and 5000 in the United States through its pharmacy network.

Despite the seemingly unstoppable Wal-Mart juggernaut, companies like Jean Coutu Group prove that other retailers can continue to thrive and grow with a mixture of targeted marketing and "hometown" service.

Jean Coutu Group is listed on the Montreal and Toronto stock exchanges.

Revenue Growth: ★★★★
Past five years: 16 percent

Pre-tax Income Growth: ★★★★
Past five years: 15 percent

Total Return: ★★★★★
Past five years: 29 percent

Return on Capital Employed: 0
Past five years: 3 percent

Jean Coutu Group (PJC) Inc. at a Glance

Fiscal year ended: May 1999

Revenue and net income in $ millions

	1995	1996	1997	1998	1999	4-Year Growth Average (%)	4-Year Growth Total (%)
Total Revenue	1,274	1,614	1,711	1,940	2,289	16.03	79.71
Net Income	45	46	57	63	74	13.49	64.39
Earnings/ Share ($)	0.86	0.88	1.08	1.2	1.41	13.42	63.95
Dividend/ Share ($)	0.12	0.12	0.14	0.16	0.2	13.99	66.67
Dividend Yield (%)	1.35	1.39	1	0.67	0.84	–	–
Price to Earnings (PE)	10.32	9.83	13.01	19.79	16.84	–	–

Stock Growth (High-Low-Close)

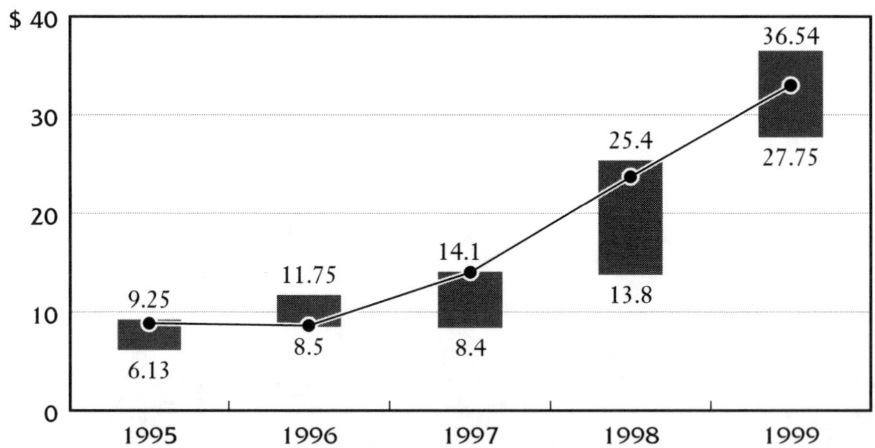

Close	8.88	8.65	14.05	23.75	33.00

32

LEITCH TECHNOLOGY CORP.

25 Dyas Road
North York, ON M3B 1V7
(416) 445-9640
www.leitch.com

Chairman, CEO: Robert A. Lehtonen
President, COO: Frederick L. Godard

Revenue Growth	★★★★★
Pre-tax Income Growth	★★★★★
Total Return	★★★★
Return on Capital Employed	–★
TSE: LTV	**13**

Leitch Technology Corporation designs, manufactures, and sells digital and analog hardware and software for the television broadcast and production markets. The company is also extending its product lines to include video transmission over the Internet and other telecommunications markets.

The move towards digital delivery of television signals may represent the single largest hardware upgrade of the next decade. While the ubiquity of the personal computer and cell phone is essentially a late twentieth century phenomenon, television has long been a household fixture. Given the complexity, scope, and cost of upgrading this technology, the digitization of mainstream TV broadcasting has been slower to take hold than might have originally been expected. Having said this, companies like Leitch are well positioned to ride the wave when it finally picks up steam.

For fiscal 1999 (year ending April 30, 1999), revenue was $173 million, versus $148 million in fiscal 1998. For the first nine months of fiscal 2000 (ending January 31, 2000), revenue amounted to $124 million, versus $137 million for the same period a year earlier.

During fiscal 1999, Leitch's sales were geographically distributed as follows: 50 percent in the United States, 26 percent in Europe, 12 percent in Canada, 6 percent in Asia, and 6 percent elsewhere.

The company reports that its client base is broad, with no single customer accounting for more than 10 percent of its revenue. Leitch probably represents one of the best Canadian technology companies that have yet to experience their best growth period.

Leitch is headquartered in Toronto, with offices and facilities in the United States, the UK, Brazil, Japan, Hong Kong, Australia, Germany, and Sweden. The company employs approximately 700 people worldwide.

Leitch is listed as part of the TSE 300 index.

Revenue Growth: ★★★★★

Past five years: 33 percent

Pre-tax Income Growth: ★★★★★

Past five years: 29 percent

Total Return: ★★★★

Past five years: 18 percent

Return on Capital Employed: –★

Past five years: –2 percent

Leitch Technology Corp. at a Glance

Fiscal year ended: April 2000

Revenue and net income in $ millions

						4-Year Growth	
	1995	1996	1997	1998	1999	Average (%)	Total (%)
Total Revenue	57	76	118	148	173	32.95	205.08
Net Income	10	13	20	23	26	27.69	158.39
Earnings/ Share ($)	0.455	0.56	0.82	0.89	0.98	22.04	115.38
Dividend/ Share ($)	0	0	0	0	0	–	–
Dividend Yield (%)	0	0	0	0	0	–	–
Price to Earnings (PE)	24.73	32.37	35.67	32.58	26.58	–	–

Stock Growth (High-Low-Close)

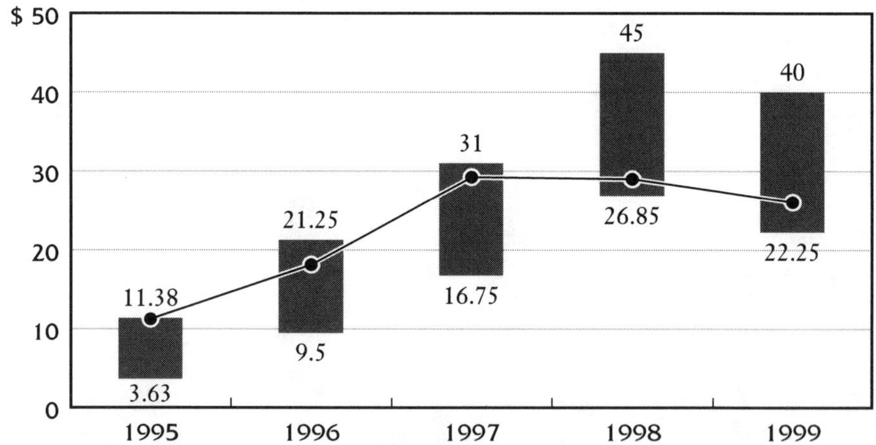

	1995	1996	1997	1998	1999
Close	11.25	18.13	29.25	29	26.05

33

MDS INC.

100 International Boulevard
Toronto, ON M9W 6J6
(416) 675-7661
www.mdsintl.com

President, CEO: J.A. Rogers

Revenue Growth	★★★
Pre-tax Income Growth	★★★★★
Total Return	★★★★★
Return on Capital Employed	0
TSE: MDS	**13**

Most Canadians' lives have been touched in one way or another by MDS. The company's growth has exploded over the last ten years. Governments across the globe must tackle the challenges of managing their health care systems in the face of aging populations. Just as a lot of corporations have looked at outsourcing more of what they do, so too have hospitals and other health care service providers. MDS Inc. is an international health care products and services company. Its business is divided into two segments: Health and Life Sciences.

Consolidated revenue for fiscal 1999 (year ending October 31, 1999) was $1.2 billion, versus $1 billion in fiscal 1998, an increase of 19 percent. The geographical division of revenue was 43 percent from Canada, 34 percent U.S., and 23 percent international.

The Health segment provides diagnostic laboratory information and related services, laboratory management through joint ventures, medical-product and anesthesia distribution services, and anesthesia equipment for dental and veterinary use. This segment's customers are principally health care professionals and health care institutions such as hospitals.

In fiscal 1999 the Health segment accounted for revenue of $589 million, versus $551 million in fiscal 1998.

The Life Sciences segment provides drug-development research and related services on a contract basis, medical-device and consumer-product sterilization, medical isotopes, radiation-therapy and cancer-treatment products and systems, and analytical instruments and testing services. This segment's customers are principally health care institutions such as hospitals, biotechnology and pharmaceutical companies, and medical-product companies.

In fiscal 1999 the Life Sciences segment accounted for $603 million, versus $451 million in fiscal 1998.

For the first quarter of fiscal 2000 (three months ending January 31, 2000) the company reported revenue of $312 million ($145 million from the Health segment, $168 million from the Life Sciences segment). This represents a 15 percent increase over the same quarter in the previous year.

In the same way that oil services companies represent a "safer" way of investing in that industry without the exploration risk, MDS provides investors with a way to take advantage of emerging biotechnology without the billions of dollars and all of the concomitant research risk that goes with drug and therapy development.

MDS Inc. is headquartered in Toronto and employs approximately 8500 people worldwide.

Revenue Growth: ★★★

Past five years: 14.8 percent

Pre-tax Income Growth: ★★★★★

Past five years: 27 percent

Total Return: ★★★★★

Past five years: 41 percent

Return on Capital Employed: 0

Past five years: 4 percent

MDS Inc. at a Glance

Fiscal year ended: October 1999

Revenue and net income in $ millions

	1995	1996	1997	1998	1999	4-Year Growth Average (%)	4-Year Growth Total (%)
Total Revenue	689	819	930	1,001	1,192	14.77	72.9
Net Income	35	51	65	58	86	27.36	143.16
Earnings/ Share ($)	0.67	0.93	1.15	1.02	1.47	23.82	119.4
Dividend/ Share ($)	0.088	0.1	0.113	0.128	0.142	12.71	61.36
Dividend Yield (%)	0.89	0.54	0.35	0.45	0.51	–	–
Price to Earnings (PE)	14.74	20.05	28.3	27.94	19.05	–	–

Stock Growth (High-Low-Close)

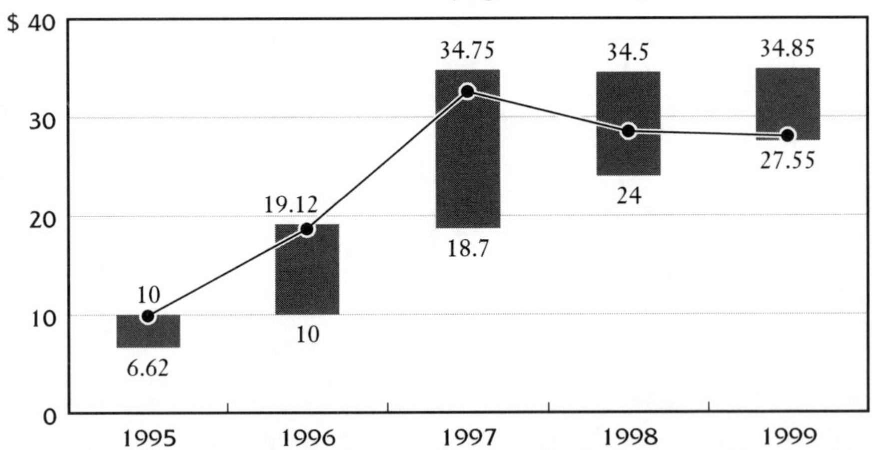

Close	9.87	18.65	32.55	28.5	28

34

BOMBARDIER INC.

800 René-Lévesque West, 29th Floor
Montreal, Quebec H3B 1Y8
(514) 861-9481
www.bombardier.com

President, Chairman, CEO: Laurent Beaudoin

Revenue Growth	★★★★
Pre-tax Income Growth	★★★★★
Total Return	★★★★★
Return on Capital Employed	–★
TSE: BBD.B	**13**

Bombardier has evolved over the last 50 years into a diversified transportation equipment company. Today, more investors associate the company with its aerospace business than with its Ski-Doo roots. The company has proven to be adept at recognizing trends earlier than its rivals and arguably has established trends with its foresight—the Regional Jet program being a recent example of the latter.

Because Bombardier is one of the few large manufacturing companies in Canada, it has been the recipient of considerable government largesse through such programs as Technology Partnerships Canada, an arm of Industry Canada. Bombardier argues that these are not subsidies, merely tax incentives to keep work in Canada, but these programs have landed Bombardier in an ongoing dispute with its Brazilian rival, Embraer. These types of inter-company conflict are nothing new to the global aerospace business and in many ways can be viewed as simply the cost of doing business.

Bombardier is a truly global company, employing more than 52,000 people worldwide. Over 90 percent of its revenue ($11.5 billion for the year ending January 31, 1999) is derived from sales outside Canada. The company maintains production facilities in North and Central America, Europe, Scandinavia, and China.

The company is organized into five major groups:

- Recreational Products—all-terrain and utility vehicles, sport boats and Sea-Doo watercraft, and the world-famous Ski-Doo and Lynx snowmobiles.
- Aerospace—business, regional, and amphibious aircraft, including such trademarks as LearJet, as well as commercial and defence aviation services.
- Transportation—passenger rail vehicles, freight wagons, and transit systems, plus related services.
- Bombardier Capital—financial services, including commercial and industrial, mortgage, consumer, inventory, and technology financing.
- Bombardier International—an international sales-development group (established in 1998–99) that supports the manufacturing groups in markets outside North America and Europe.

The Aerospace group accounts for the lion's share of revenue: $6.4 billion for the year ending January 31, 1999. Meanwhile, the company's Recreational Products group has experienced slackening sales of winter vehicles due to late snowfalls in North America, as well as a drop in demand for watercraft sales.

Demand for Bombardier products is strong overall, however, with the company reporting a $25.5 billion confirmed order backlog as of January 31, 1999, a 41 percent increase over the previous year.

Bombardier remains a core portfolio holding for Canadian investors. The company has successfully diversified its business over the years and gives investors a proxy for the global economy given its reach in foreign markets. The long-term fundamentals of the markets that Bombardier serves are strong and should ensure the company's continued financial outperformance.

Bombardier was founded in 1942 and has been listed on the Toronto and Montreal stock exchanges since 1969.

Revenue Growth: ★★★★

Past five years: 18 percent

Pre-tax Income Growth: ★★★★★

Past five years: 40 percent

Total Return: ★★★★★

Past five years: 38 percent

Return on Capital Employed: –★

Past five years: –1 percent

Bombardier Inc. at a Glance

Fiscal year ended: January 2000

Revenue and net income in $ millions

	1995	1996	1997	1998	1999	4-Year Growth Average (%)	4-Year Growth Total (%)
Total Revenue	5,953	7,123	7,975	8,508	11,500	18.42	93.51
Net Income	247	158	406	420	554	39.07	124.02
Earnings/ Share ($)	0.345	0.225	0.58	0.58	0.76	38.51	120.29
Dividend/ Share ($)	0.078	0.103	0.103	0.153	0.173	23.42	121.79
Dividend Yield (%)	1.37	1.04	0.79	1.09	0.77	–	–
Price to Earnings (PE)	16.49	44.17	22.41	24.22	29.61	–	–

Stock Growth (High-Low-Close)

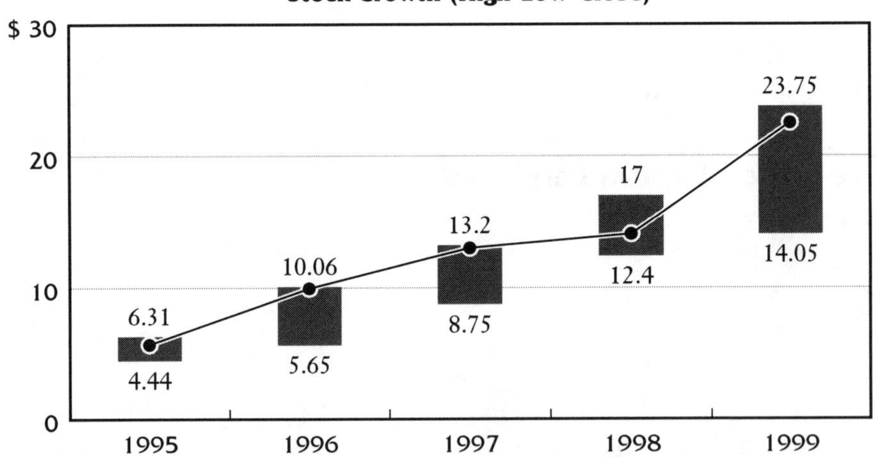

Close	5.69	9.94	13	14.05	22.5

35

LEON'S FURNITURE LTD.

45 Gordon Mackay Road, Box 1100, Station "B"
Weston, ON M9L 2R8
(416) 243-7880

Chairman, CEO: Anthony Thomas Leon
President, CEO: Mark Joseph Leon

Revenue Growth	★
Pre-tax Income Growth	★★★★★
Total Return	★★★
Return on Capital Employed	★★★
TSE: LNF	**12**

Perhaps best known for the cutting-edge humour of its television ads, Leon's Furniture Ltd. operates the largest chain of furniture warehouse stores across Canada. The company also sells consumer electronics and major appliances. While a number of other "big-box" retailers have emerged in recent years, Leon's has been a pioneer in this area. Its innovative marketing and finance programs have kept the chain relevant in a time of brutal competition.

Founded in 1909, this company has thrived under the leadership of successive generations of the Leon family. Obviously this is no small feat when juxtaposed with the end of a very famous Eaton family retail dynasty in 1999. While the company's five-year total return is a respectable 14.5 percent, this must disappoint the Leons given that the growth in pre-tax and net income has been better than 20 percent annually. The company's financial performance is particularly stellar in terms of return on invested capital—never below 20 percent over the last five years.

As of the end of fiscal 1998 (year ending December 31, 1998) the company had 46 outlets, 23 of which were franchises and 3 of which were leased operations; the remainder were company-owned. The company opened new superstores in Barrie and London during 1999 and has plans to open further superstores in Montreal, Red Deer, and St. Catharines in 2000.

In fiscal 1999 the company reported revenue of $371 million, versus $337 million in fiscal 1998, a 10 percent increase.

In July 1999 the company announced that it had sold the second of its two Arizona properties; the first was sold in 1998. The company's Arizona operations were discontinued in mid-1997.

Leon's corporate offices are based in Weston, Ontario, and its stock is listed on the Toronto Stock Exchange.

Revenue Growth: ★

Past five years: 7 percent

Pre-tax Income Growth: ★ ★ ★ ★ ★

Past five years: 20 percent

Total Return: ★ ★ ★

Past five years: 14.5 percent

Return on Capital Employed: ★ ★ ★

Past five years: 11 percent

Leon's Furniture Ltd. at a Glance

Fiscal year ended: December 1999

Revenue and net income in $ millions

						4-Year Growth	
	1995	1996	1997	1998	1999	Average (%)	Total (%)
Total Revenue	283	289	316	337	371	7.08	31.26
Net Income	17	18	22	26	36	20.96	109.56
Earnings/ Share ($)	0.84	0.86	1.05	1.27	1.73	20.41	105.95
Dividend/ Share ($)	0.2	0.7	0.22	0.27	0.81	101.04	305
Dividend Yield (%)	1.57	5.38	1.01	1.56	3.28	–	–
Price to Earnings (PE)	15.18	15.12	20.71	13.66	14.28	–	–

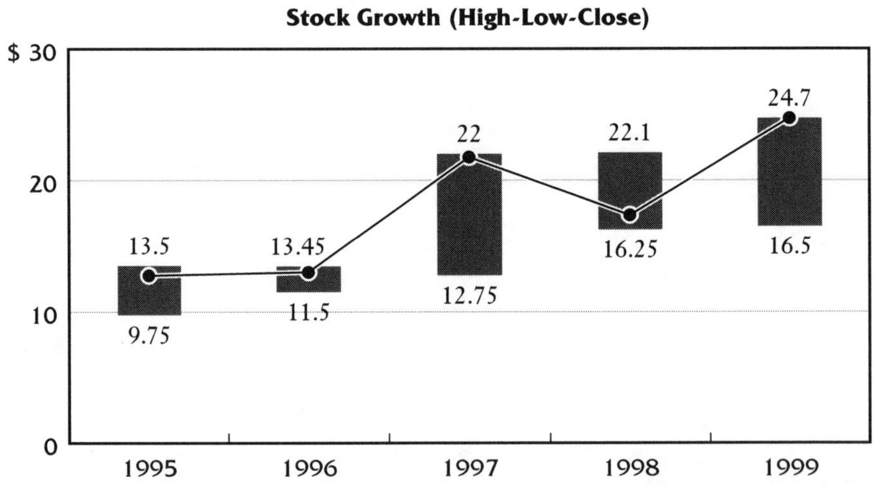

Close	12.75	13	21.75	17.35	24.7

36

BCE INC.

1000 de la Gauchetière West, Suite 3700
Montreal, PQ H3B 4Y7
(800) 339-6353
www.bce.ca

Chairman, CEO: L.R. Wilson
President, COO: J.C. Monty

Revenue Growth	–★
Pre-tax Income Growth	★★★★★
Total Return	★★★
Return on Capital Employed	★★★★★
TSE: BCE	**12**

Most people think of BCE as the "phone company." It is, but it is also much more than that. BCE is really a holding company that gives investors a diverse play in one of the fundamental pillars of the economy: telecommunications services and hardware.

As a "holding" company, BCE has investments in the following core areas:

- Wired and wireless telephone networks, principally through Bell Canada and Bell Mobility

- Internet protocol (IP)-based networks and solutions
- Electronic commerce
- Systems integration
- Directories
- Satellite networks
- High-speed Internet access
- Web hosting
- Direct-to-home entertainment

BCE operates in 150 countries and ranks as one of Canada's largest corporations with over $14 billion in revenue and over 50,000 employees.

BCE has extended its reach from a basic telephony company into a multi-faceted communications and technology company. Alliances, cross-investments, and mergers now drive the international telecommunications market and BCE is an active participant, with relationships spanning MCI, Ameritech, and a host of smaller ventures.

Any discussion of BCE has to include Nortel Networks. Nortel is arguably *the* Canadian high-tech success story. What began as the manufacturing arm of Bell Canada has emerged as one of the world's leading suppliers of telecommunications equipment. Its products are integral to basic telephony infrastructure, inter- and intra-business networks, and high-speed data networks. In the spring of 2000, BCE "spun off" most of its Nortel stock to BCE stockholders, passing on Nortel's incredible success directly to their hands and unlocking the value of BCE's non-Nortel holdings. As a result, BCE no longer has any significant connection to Nortel.

However, even with Nortel, BCE constitutes an Internet "play" in many aspects of its business. It is a company with revenue and earnings, however—a relatively scarce commodity in the Internet world. Having outperformed the TSE 300 in seven of the last ten years and paying a solid dividend, BCE remains a must for virtually every portfolio.

BCE is currently listed on the Toronto, Montreal, New York, and London stock exchanges.

Revenue Growth: −★

Past five years: –8 percent

Pre-tax Income Growth: ★★★★★

Past five years: 34 percent

Total Return: ★★★

Past five years: 13 percent

Return on Capital Employed: ★★★★★

Past five years: 26 percent

BCE Inc. at a Glance

Fiscal year ended: December 1999

Revenue and net income in $ millions

	1995	1996	1997	1998	1999	4-Year Growth Average (%)	4-Year Growth Total (%)
Total Revenue	24,624	28,167	34,517	27,454	14,214	–7.99	–42.09
Net Income	782	1,152	1,414	4,598	5,459	78.49	598.08
Earnings/ Share ($)	1.12	1.7	2.11	7.07	8.35	82.27	645.54
Dividend/ Share ($)	1.36	1.36	1.36	1.36	1.36	–	0
Dividend Yield (%)	5.76	4.17	2.85	2.35	1.04	–	–
Price to Earnings (PE)	21.09	19.21	22.58	8.18	15.71	–	–

Stock Growth (High-Low-Close)

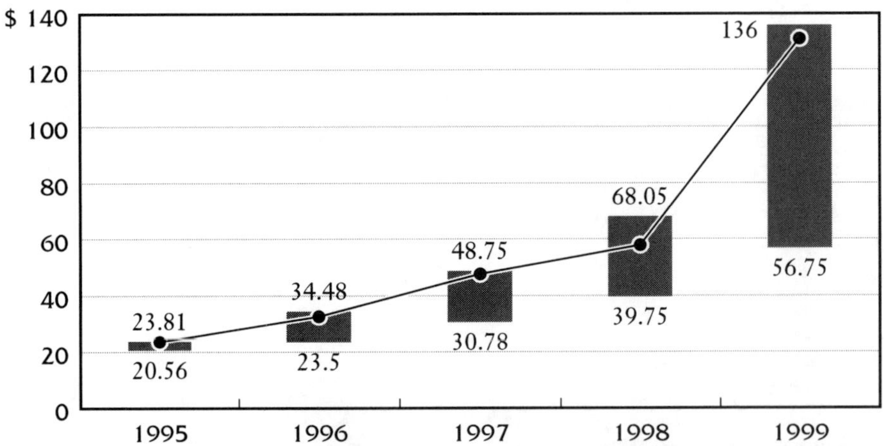

	1995	1996	1997	1998	1999
Close	23.63	32.65	47.65	57.85	131.15

37

MAPLE LEAF FOODS INC.

30 St. Clair Avenue West, Suite 1500
Toronto, ON M4V 3A2
(416) 926-2000

President, COO: M.H. McCain
Vice Chairman, CEO: A.D. McLean

Revenue Growth	0
Pre-tax Income Growth	★★★★★
Total Return	★★
Return on Capital Employed	★★★★★
TSE: MFI	**12**

Maple Leaf Foods Inc. is Canada's largest food-processing company. The company's business is divided into three segments: Meat Products Group, Bakery Products Group, and Agribusiness Group.

The Meat Products Group consists of Maple Leaf Consumer Foods (prepared meats), Maple Leaf Pork (fresh and frozen pork products), Maple Leaf Poultry (fresh and frozen chicken and turkey products), and Maple Leaf Foods International (the largest global food-marketing and -distribution operation in Canada, according to the company).

The Bakery Products Group consists of Maple Leaf Bakery U.S.A. and 68 percent ownership of Canada Bread Company Ltd., both of which produce bakery products.

The Agribusiness Group consists of Shur-Gain (livestock feed and pet food) and Rothsay Rendering (tallow and protein products from animal waste and food by-product recycling).

In October 1999 the company acquired The Landmark Group Inc., which consists of Landmark Feeds (the largest livestock feed company in western Canada) and Elite Swine (western Canada's largest hog genetics and marketing organization), for $140 million. This acquisition gives Maple Leaf a 30 percent share of the Canadian animal-feed and -nutrition market.

In late 1999 the company sold its 61.5 percent ownership of Canbrands International, a cat-litter manufacturer.

Revenue for fiscal 1999 (year ending December 31, 1999) was $3.6 billion, versus $3.3 billion in fiscal 1998. In fiscal 1999 the Meat Products Group accounted for $2.1 billion, the Agribusiness Group for $741 million, and the Bakery Products Group for $676 million.

The company reported export sales for fiscal 1999 to be $697 million, versus $643 million in fiscal 1998.

Maple Leaf Foods is headquartered in Toronto and employs approximately 11,000 people.

Revenue Growth: 0

Past five years: 4 percent

Pre-tax Income Growth: ★★★★★

Past five years: 273 percent

Total Return: ★★

Past five years: 9 percent

Return on Capital Employed: ★★★★★

Past five years: 269 percent

Maple Leaf Foods Inc. at a Glance

Fiscal year ended: December 1999

Revenue and net income in $ millions

	1995	1996	1997	1998	1999	4-Year Growth Average (%)	4-Year Growth Total (%)
Total Revenue	3,068	3,210	3,678	3,281	3,551	4.17	15.76
Net Income	–43	42	47	–23	77	122.51	276.55
Earnings/ Share ($)	–0.52	0.45	0.51	–0.25	0.75	112.71	244.23
Dividend/ Share ($)	0.215	0.16	0.16	0.16	0.16	–6.4	–25.58
Dividend Yield (%)	3.51	1.73	1.01	1.08	1.14	–	–
Price to Earnings (PE)	N/A	20.56	30.98	N/A	18.67	–	–

Stock Growth (High-Low-Close)

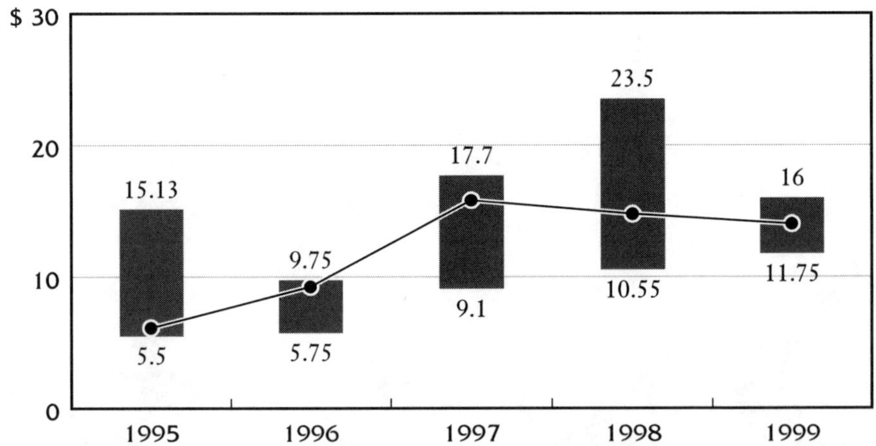

Close	6.13	9.25	15.8	14.75	14

38

ROYAL GROUP TECHNOLOGIES INC.

1 Royal Gate Boulevard
Woodbridge, ON L4L 8Z7
(905) 264-0701
www.royplas.com

President, Chairman, CEO: Vic De Zen

Revenue Growth	★★★★★
Pre-tax Income Growth	★★★★★
Total Return	★★★
Return on Capital Employed	–★
TSE: RYG	**12**

Royal Group Technologies Ltd. manufactures polymer-based products used in home construction and renovation. The company's business is divided into two operating segments: Products and Support. The company's founder, Vic De Zen, has been called the Frank Stronach of building products. Both Royal Group Technologies and Magna International started as one-man operations and grew through acquisition, and both have come to dominate their respective industries.

As of February 1, 2000, the Products segment was made up of more than 80 wholly owned or joint-ventured businesses, primarily in Canada, the United States, and Mexico; the company also has operations in South America, Europe, and Asia. The Products segment is organized as follows:

- Home Improvement Products is responsible for the manufacture of extruded poly vinyl chloride (PVC) products, such as fencing, decking, siding, and residential doors. These products are sold to fabricators and distributors specializing in renovation.
- Consumer Products is responsible for extruded and injection-molded products, such as window coverings, indoor and outdoor storage, and patio furniture. These products are sold to home-owners through retail stores.
- Construction Products is responsible for a trademarked, pre-engineered, component-based building system, The Royal Building System, used in residential, commercial, industrial, institutional, and agricultural construction. This sub-segment is also responsible for the manufacture of pipes and fittings. These products are sold to developers, contractors, and other distributors.

The Support segment provides materials (resins, chemicals, and recycling), equipment (machinery and manufacturing systems), real estate services (plant design and property management), and logistical support (transportation) to the Products segment.

In fiscal 1999 (year ending September 30, 1999) the company reported revenue of $1.3 billion, of which Home Improvement Products accounted for $662 million, Consumer Products for $350 million, and Construction Products for $229 million. Revenue in fiscal 1998 was $1.1 billion.

For the first quarter of fiscal 2000 (three months ending December 31, 1999) the company reported revenue of $320 million, versus $261 million for the same period one year earlier, a 23 percent increase.

Royal Group Technologies is headquartered in Woodbridge, Ontario, and has approximately 7500 direct and indirect employees.

The company's shares are traded on the Toronto and New York stock exchanges.

Revenue Growth: ★★★★★

Past five years: 24 percent

Pre-tax Income Growth: ★★★★★

Past five years: 33 percent

Total Return: ★★★

Past five years: 13 percent

Return on Capital Employed: –★

Past five years: –2 percent

Royal Group Technologies Ltd. at a Glance

Fiscal year ended: September 1999

Revenue and net income in $ millions

						4-Year Growth	
	1995	1996	1997	1998	1999	Average (%)	Total (%)
Total Revenue	535	675	849	1,050	1,282	24.43	139.6
Net Income	47	67	92	116	150	34.1	221.73
Earnings/ Share ($)	0.66	0.87	1.13	1.38	1.75	27.66	165.15
Dividend/ Share ($)	0	0	0	0	0	–	–
Dividend Yield (%)	0	0	0	0	0	–	–
Price to Earnings (PE)	26.7	26.72	34.82	18.73	18.03	–	–

Stock Growth (High-Low-Close)

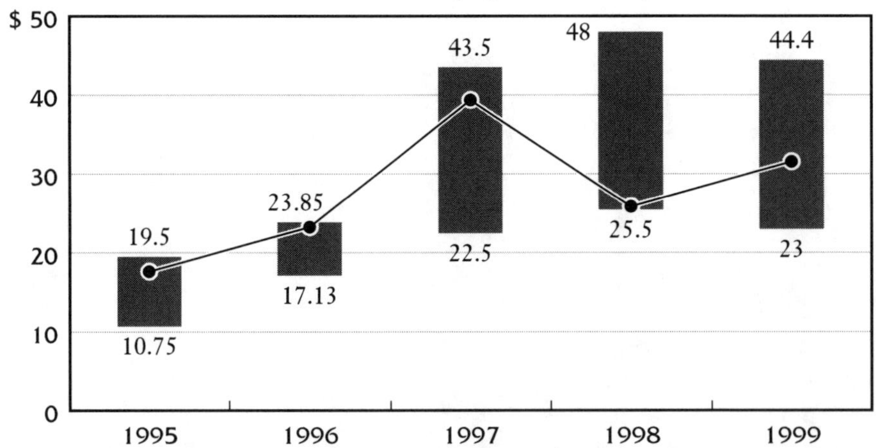

	1995	1996	1997	1998	1999
Close	17.63	23.25	39.35	25.85	31.55

39

IMPERIAL OIL LTD.

111 St. Clair Avenue West
Toronto, ON M5W 1K3
(800) 567-3776
www.imperialoil.ca

Chairman, President, CEO: R.B. Peterson

Revenue Growth	0
Pre-tax Income Growth	★ ★ ★
Total Return	★ ★ ★ ★ ★
Return on Capital Employed	★ ★ ★ ★
TSE: IMO	**12**

Imperial Oil Ltd. is Canada's largest crude-oil producer, as well as its largest refiner and marketer of petroleum products (under the Esso banner). The company also produces natural gas and petrochemicals.

The company's business is organized into three segments: Natural Resources, Petroleum Products, and Chemicals.

The Natural Resources segment is responsible for the company's natural resource operations, including crude-oil and natural gas production and the company's oil sands operations.

The Petroleum Products segment is responsible for the company's nationwide chain of approximately 2500 Esso service stations (both company- and dealer-owned or leased), as well as the company's refineries. Imperial Oil sold almost 76 million litres of petroleum products (such as gasoline, heating oil, and lube oils) per day in 1999.

The Chemicals segment is responsible for the company's chemical manufacturing operation in Sarnia, Ontario, as well as a Canada-wide series of distribution centres. During 1999 the company sold approximately 3 tonnes of petrochemicals (such as polyethylene and benzene) per day.

Consolidated revenue for fiscal 1999 (year ending December 31, 1999) was $10.3 billion, versus $9.1 billion in fiscal 1998. Revenue from the Petroleum Products segment accounted for $8.4 billion in fiscal 1999 (versus $7.4 billion in fiscal 1998), Natural Resources accounted for $2.8 billion (versus $2 billion), and Chemicals accounted for $730 million (versus $865 million).*

At the end of 1999 the company reported net proved crude-oil and liquids reserves (developed and undeveloped) of approximately 1.7 billion barrels, and natural gas reserves of 1.7 billion cubic feet.

The corporate headquarters for Imperial Oil is located in Toronto. The company employs approximately 6600 people full time.

ExxonMobil Corporation owns approximately 70 percent of Imperial Oil's shares.

---

* Note: the divisional revenue figures do not add up to the consolidated revenue figure due to the exclusion of intersegment sales from the consolidated figure.

Revenue Growth: 0

Past five years: 3 percent

Pre-tax Income Growth: ★ ★ ★

Past five years: 13 percent

Total Return: ★ ★ ★ ★ ★

Past five years: 20 percent

Return on Capital Employed: ★ ★ ★ ★

Past five years: 18 percent

Imperial Oil Ltd. at a Glance

Fiscal year ended: December 1999

Revenue and net income in $ millions

						4-Year Growth	
	1995	1996	1997	1998	1999	Average (%)	Total (%)
Total Revenue	9,600	10,501	11,122	9,145	10,348	2.67	7.79
Net Income	514	786	847	554	582	7.79	13.23
Earnings/ Share ($)	0.89	1.49	1.83	1.26	1.35	16.56	51.69
Dividend/ Share ($)	0.633	0.683	0.733	0.74	0.75	4.38	18.48
Dividend Yield (%)	3.85	3.18	2.39	3.01	2.42	–	–
Price to Earnings (PE)	18.49	14.43	16.76	19.48	22.96	–	–

Stock Growth (High-Low-Close)

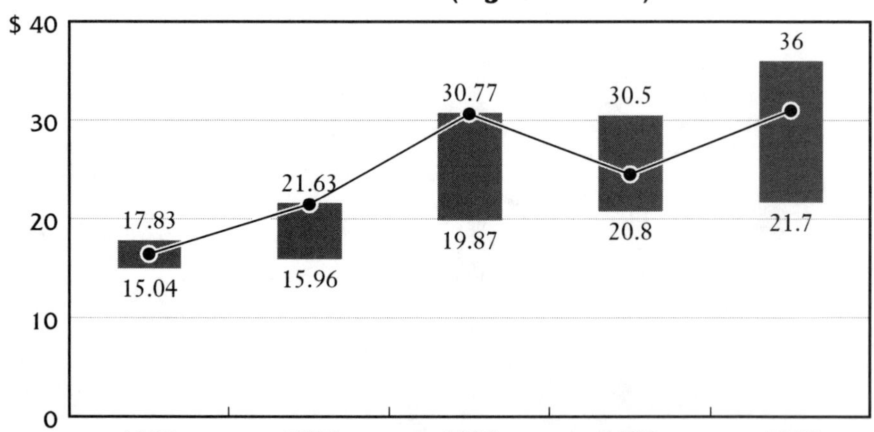

	1995	1996	1997	1998	1999
Close	16.46	21.5	30.67	24.55	31

40

INTERTAPE POLYMER GROUP INC.

110E Montée de Liesse
St. Laurent, PQ H4T 1N4
(514) 731-0731
www.intertapepolymer.com

Chairman, CEO: M.F. Yull

Revenue Growth	★★★★★
Pre-tax Income Growth	★★★★★
Total Return	★★
Return on Capital Employed	−★
TSE: ITP	**11**

Intertape Polymer Group manufactures specialized plastic and paper products; it also manufactures related packaging systems. Examples of the company's products include carton-sealing equipment and packaging products, such as shrink wrap, and specialty tapes, such as duct tape, as well as woven, coated fabrics, returnable produce containers, and soft-drink transport and display cases.

The company has maintained a blistering growth rate for the last several years, combining organic growth with a shrewd acquisition record. Unlike a lot of other plastics companies, whose earnings records are spotty due to swings in commodity prices and raw material costs, Intertape has faired quite well in controlling its cost structure. This allows the company to really leverage its revenue growth.

In fiscal 1998 (year ending December 31, 1998) the company reported sales of $579 million, versus $348 million in fiscal 1997, a 66 percent increase. The company attributed this rise in sales to lower unit selling prices, as well as to recent acquisitions: American Tape Company, which manufactures a wide variety of tape and packaging products, in late 1997; and Rexford Paper Company, a water-activated tape manufacturer and packaging-products distributor, and Anchor Continental, a pressure-sensitive tape manufacturer, in 1998.

In the first three-quarters of fiscal 1999 the company reported sales of $416 million, versus $256 million for the same nine-month period in fiscal 1998. The company also continued to make strategic acquisitions in 1999: Central Products Company and Spinnaker Electrical Tape Company, both of which manufacture industrial and specialty tapes.

The company is headquartered in Montreal and employs approximately 2400 people. It has 13 manufacturing facilities across North America.

Intertape Polymer Group is listed on the Toronto and New York stock exchanges.

Revenue Growth: ★★★★★

Past five years: 44 percent

Pre-tax Income Growth: ★★★★★

Past five years: 31 percent

Total Return: ★★

Past five years: 9 percent

Return on Capital Employed: –★

Past five years: –2 percent

Intertape Polymer Group Inc. at a Glance

Fiscal year ended: December 1999

Revenue and net income in US$ millions

	1995	1996	1997	1998	1999	4-Year Growth Average (%)	4-Year Growth Total (%)
Total Revenue	225	271	348	579	828	43.95	312.23
Net Income	22	29	14	44	12	38.96	–38.75
Earnings/ Share ($)	0.97	1.13	0.53	1.68	0.421	31.91	–51.33
Dividend/ Share ($)	0.07	0.085	0.1	0.13	0.154	25.31	144.44
Dividend Yield (%)	0.33	0.27	0.33	0.33	0.39	–	–
Price to Earnings (PE)	22.1	27.38	58.02	23.21	93.82	–	–

Stock Growth (High-Low-Close)

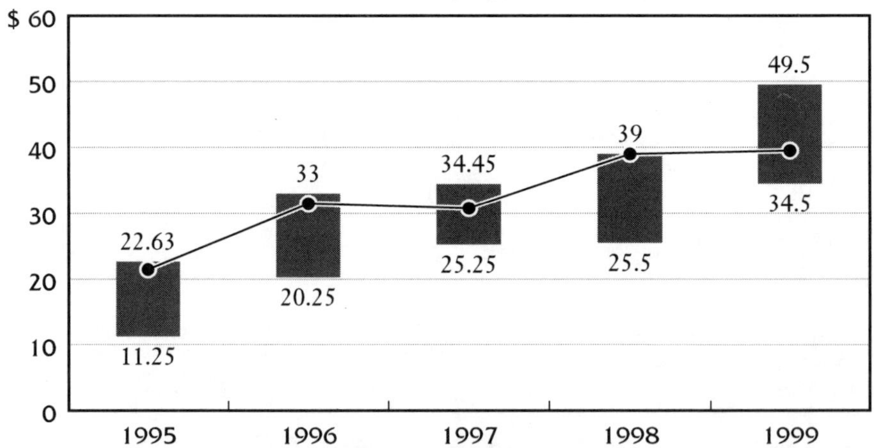

Close	21.44	31.45	30.75	39	39.5

41

UNICAN SECURITY SYSTEMS LTD.

7301 Decarie Boulevard
Montreal, PQ H4P 2G7
(514) 735-5411
www.unicangroup.com

Chairman, CEO: Aaron M. Fish
President, COO: Maurice Andrien, Jr.

Revenue Growth	★★★★★
Pre-tax Income Growth	★★★★
Total Return	★★★
Return on Capital Employed	–★
TSE: UCS.B	**11**

Unican Security Systems Ltd. manufactures and sells security products, including key blanks, key-cutting and -duplicating machines, electronic access-control systems, mechanical push-button locks, and safe and vault locks, as well as zinc die-cast hardware. The company controls an international group of subsidiaries, with operations in Canada, the United States, Italy, France, Germany, Switzerland, England, Mexico, Hungary, and Australia.

Revenue for fiscal 1999 (year ending June 30, 1999) was $478 million, versus $400 million in fiscal 1998. For the first six months of fiscal 2000 (ending December 31, 1999) the company reported revenue of $231 million, versus $229 million for the same period in the previous year.

By product line, the company's sales for fiscal 1999 were 47.7 percent keys and key machines, 27.8 percent access control, 6 percent brass cylinders, 5.9 percent contract hardware (die-casting and electroplating), and 5.1 percent vault and safe locks, with the remaining 7.5 percent coming from other businesses.

The company sells its products in over 150 countries. Its customers range from locksmith suppliers and original equipment manufacturers to the automotive and hotel industries. More than 90 percent of Unican's revenue comes from outside Canada, with the United States representing the largest market, accounting for approximately $250 million (52 percent) in fiscal 1999.

The company holds approximately 60 patents and 50 trademarks.

Notable recent acquisitions include the manufacturing assets of Productos Metalicos Alba, Mexico's largest manufacturer of key blanks, and Mauer Group, a German lock manufacturer, including locks for safety deposit boxes and coin-operated lockers.

Unican is headquartered in Montreal and employs approximately 3800 people.

The company is listed on the Toronto and Montreal stock exchanges.

Revenue Growth: ★★★★★

Past five years: 25 percent

Pre-tax Income Growth: ★★★★

Past five years: 19.8 percent

Total Return: ★★★

Past five years: 11 percent

Return on Capital Employed: –★

Past five years: –5 percent

Unican Security Systems Ltd. at a Glance

Fiscal year ended: June 1999

Revenue and net income in $ millions

	1995	1996	1997	1998	1999	4-Year Growth Average (%)	4-Year Growth Total (%)
Total Revenue	199	240	303	400	478	24.55	139.84
Net Income	14	18	15	23	25	17.61	76.88
Earnings/ Share ($)	0.82	0.99	0.8	1.16	1.21	12.71	47.56
Dividend/ Share ($)	0.084	0.096	0.102	0.102	0.114	8.08	35.71
Dividend Yield (%)	0.65	0.44	0.37	0.3	0.36	–	–
Price to Earnings (PE)	15.78	21.87	34.75	29.4	26.45	–	–

Stock Growth (High-Low-Close)

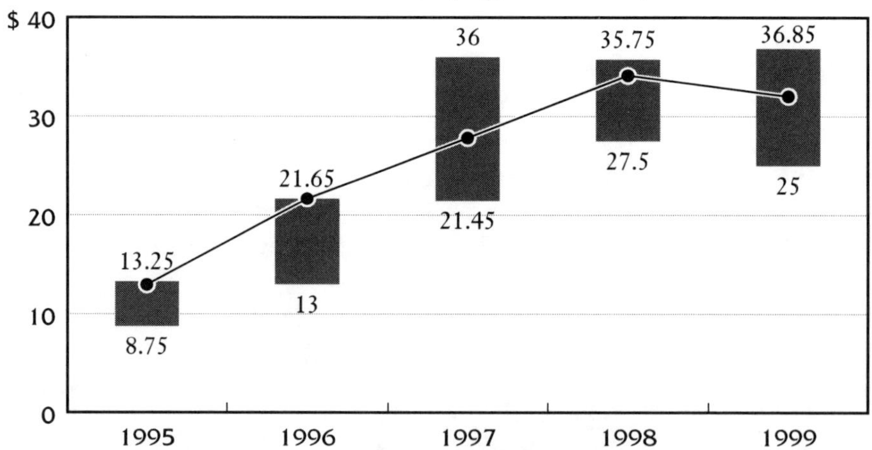

Close	12.94	21.65	27.8	34.1	32

42

BRASCAN CORP.

181 Bay Street, Suite 4440
Toronto, ON M5J 2T3
(416) 363-9491
www.edperbrascan.com

President, CEO: Jack L. Cockwell
Executive Chairman: Robert J. Harding

Revenue Growth	–★
Pre-tax Income Growth	★★★★★
Total Return	★★★★★
Return on Capital Employed	★
TSE: BNN.A	**10**

The Brascan Corporation (formerly EdperBrascan Corp., the company changed its name in spring 2000) is a diversified company with interests in the mining and metals, forestry products, real estate, energy, and finance industries in North America and South America.

The company's business is organized as follows:

- Natural Resource Operations—This segment consists of 40 percent ownership of Noranda Inc., the world's largest custom copper smelter, as well as the third-largest producer of both nickel and mined zinc; and 31 percent ownership of Nexfor, a pulp and paper manufacturer.

- Property Operations—This segment consists of 50 percent ownership of Brookfield Properties Corporation, which owns and operates commercial office space in North American urban centres (such as New York, Toronto, Calgary, and Boston) and develops residential communities.
- Energy Operations—This segment consists of 93 percent ownership of Great Lakes Power Inc., an independent hydroelectric power company operating in Ontario, Quebec, and the southern United States.
- Financial and Other Operations—This segment consists of 65 percent ownership of Trilon Financial Corporation, a financial services company that engages in activities such as investment banking and investment management, and 100 percent ownership of Brascan Brazil Ltd., a company that functions as a microcosm of its parent, with interests in natural resources, real-estate development, and financial services in Brazil.

The company sold its 39 percent interest in Canadian Hunter Exploration Ltd., a natural gas exploration and development company, in early 2000.

For fiscal 1999 (year ending December 31, 1999) the company reported that its share of affiliated revenue was $5.9 billion, versus $5.7 billion for fiscal 1998. For fiscal 1999 the Natural Resource Operations accounted for $3.3 billion, Property Operations accounted for $1.4 billion, Financial and Other Operations accounted for $681 million, and Energy Operations accounted for $397 million.

Brascan is headquartered in Toronto and employs approximately 50,000 people.

Revenue Growth: –★

Past five years: –6 percent

Pre-tax Income Growth: ★ ★ ★ ★ ★

Past five years: 22 percent

Total Return: ★ ★ ★ ★ ★

Past five years: 23 percent

Return on Capital Employed: ★

Past five years: 7 percent

Brascan Corp. at a Glance

Fiscal year ended: December 1999

Revenue and net income in $ millions

						3-Year Growth	
	1995	1996	1997	1998	1999	Average (%)	Total (%)
Total Revenue	–	1,595	1,357	1,409	1,310	–6.04	–17.87
Net Income	–	257	620	415	423	36.7	64.59
Earnings/ Share ($)	–	1.28	3.34	2.12	2.15	41.94	67.97
Dividend/ Share ($)	–	0.98	0.98	0.98	0.98	–	0
Dividend Yield (%)	–	4.76	3.77	4.6	5.13	–	–
Price to Earnings (PE)	–	16.09	7.78	10.05	8.88	–	–

Stock Growth (High-Low-Close)

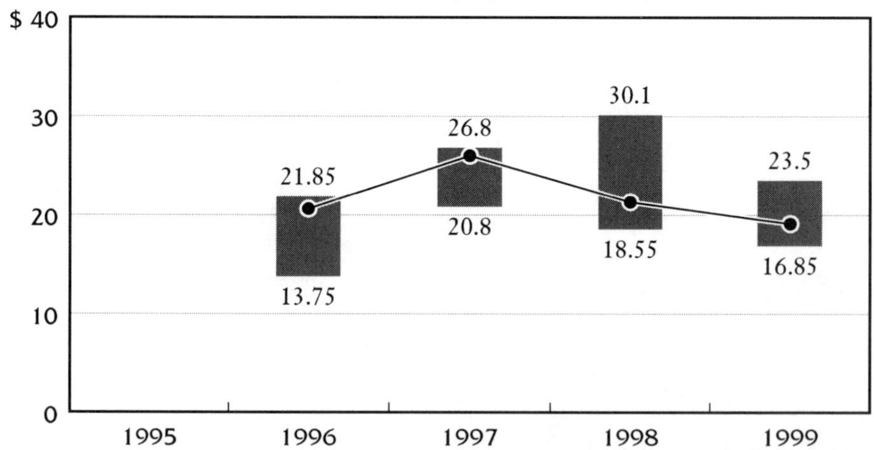

Close	1995	1996	1997	1998	1999
Close		20.6	26	21.3	19.1

43

WESCAST INDUSTRIES INC.

Box 1930, 799 Powerline Rd. W.
Brantford, ON N3T 5W5
(519) 759-0452
www.wescast.com

Chairman: Richard W. LeVan
President and CEO: Raymond T. Finnie

Revenue Growth	★★★★★
Pre-tax Income Growth	★★★★★
Total Return	–★
Return on Capital Employed	0
TSE: WCS.A	**9**

Wescast Industries Inc. is the world's largest manufacturer of exhaust manifolds for passenger cars and light trucks. The company also manufactures parts for steel pump equipment for the pulp and paper, food processing, and petrochemical industries. Wescasts's estimated share of the North American exhaust manifold market was approximately 49 percent in 1999. It provides its customers with design engineering services to compliment its manufacturing expertise.

Wescast has blazed a path of blistering growth over the last five years with average annual revenue increases in excess of 20 percent generating better than 35 percent jumps in annual income. What is perhaps even more impressive is the fact that the company has generated a better than 30 percent return on capital employed for each of the last five years. This is remarkable because manufacturing companies generally will require more capital investment to generate a revenue dollar and the automotive OEMs are not known for allowing their suppliers fat margins!

Sales for fiscal 1999 (year ending January 2, 2000) were $355 million, vs. $285 million for fiscal 1998. For the first quarter of fiscal 2000 (ending April 2, 2000), the company reported sales of $105 million, vs. $84 million for the same period a year earlier.

The company has six manufacturing facilities in Ontario, as well as 49 percent ownership of a plant in Michigan. The vast majority of the company's products are exported, with the United States accounting for approximately 95 percent of fiscal 1999 revenue and the United Kingdom for 4.8 percent. The company recently entered into a joint venture with another company profiled in this book, Linamar. The two companies plan to build an exhaust component plant in Hungary by 2001. This kind of joint venture is an outstanding way for Wescast to expand its geographic reach while mitigating the financial risk that naturally accompanies investment in these "newer" capitalist economies.

The company's shares are listed on the NASDAQ and Toronto stock exchanges.

The company is headquartered in Brantford, Ontario, and, as of the end of fiscal 1999, employed approximately 2,000 people.

Revenue Growth: ★ ★ ★ ★ ★

Past five years: 21 percent

Pre-tax Income Growth: ★ ★ ★ ★ ★

Past five years: 37 percent

Total Return: –★

Past five years: –5 percent

Return on Capital Employed: 0

Past five years: 4 percent

Wescast Industries Inc. at a Glance

Fiscal year ended: December 1999

Revenue and net income in $ millions

	1995	1996	1997	1998	1999	4-Year Growth Average (%)	4-Year Growth Total (%)
Total Revenue	167	198	229	285	355	20.78	112.36
Net Income	18	28	39	48	62	37.25	247.31
Earnings/ Share ($)	1.62	2.53	2.91	3.53	4.47	29.78	175.93
Dividend/ Share ($)	0.11	0.15	0.16	0.32	0.32	35.76	190.91
Dividend Yield (%)	–	0.47	0.41	0.71	1.02	–	–
Price to Earnings (PE)	–	12.75	13.33	12.72	6.99	–	–

Stock Growth (High-Low-Close)

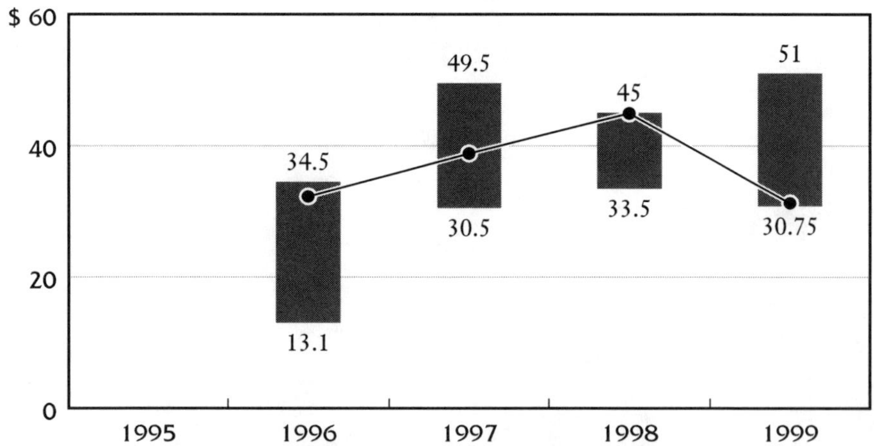

Close	1995	1996	1997	1998	1999
Close		32.25	38.8	44.9	31.25

44

ROYAL BANK OF CANADA

P.O. Box 6001
Montreal, PQ H3C 3A9
(416) 955-7803
www.royalbank.com

Chairman & CEO: J.E. Cleghorn

Revenue Growth	★
Pre-tax Income Growth	★★
Total Return	★★★★★
Return on Capital Employed	★
TSE: RY	**9**

Royal Bank of Canada (and its subsidiaries) is one of the principal financial institutions in Canada, reporting almost 10 million business and personal customers worldwide as of October 31, 1999. Its business is divided into three major segments: Personal and Commercial Banking, Royal Investment Services (formerly Wealth Management), and Corporate and Investment Banking.

Overall, Royal Bank reported gross revenue of $19.7 billion in fiscal 1999 (year ending October 31, 1999), versus $19.8 billion in fiscal 1998.

The Personal and Commercial Banking segment is responsible for personal financial services, card services, business banking, and insurance, as well as emerging financial services such as Internet banking. This segment accounted for $6.1 billion of fiscal 1999 revenue, versus $5.6 billion in fiscal 1998.

The Royal Investment Services segment is responsible for investment management, worldwide private banking, full-service brokerage services, mutual funds (Royal Bank is the second-largest mutual funds provider in Canada), and wealth management services. The company's Royal Bank Action Direct discount brokerage is the second largest in Canada. This segment accounted for fiscal 1999 revenue of $2.3 billion, versus $2.2 billion in fiscal 1998.

The Corporate and Investment Banking segment is responsible for global markets and equity, as well as investment and corporate banking services through RBC Dominion Securities. This segment accounted for fiscal 1999 revenue of $2.2 billion, versus $2 billion in fiscal 1998.

For the first quarter of fiscal 2000 (three months ending January 31, 2000) Royal Bank reported revenue of $2.8 billion (versus $2.6 billion for the same period one year earlier). Of this revenue, Personal and Commercial Banking accounted for $1.6 billion, Royal Investment Services for $640 million, and Corporate and Investment Banking for $524 million.

Headquartered in Montreal, with its chief executive offices in Toronto, Royal Bank has almost 100 offices in over 30 countries. In fiscal 1999 approximately $2 billion of the company's revenue came from international business.

Like a number of the other financial services stocks profiled in this book, Royal Bank benefits from the growth in baby boomer investment and the increasing deregulation of the Canadian and global banking systems. While long thought of as "boring old blue chips," stocks like those of the Royal Bank have started to look more like growth stocks over the last few years.

Royal Bank of Canada employs almost 52,000 people and has a network of over 1400 branches and 4500 automated banking machines.

Revenue Growth: ★
Past five years: 6 percent

Pre-tax Income Growth: ★★
Past five years: 9 percent

Total Return: ★★★★★
Past five years: 25 percent

Return on Capital Employed: ★
Past five years: 6 percent

Royal Bank of Canada at a Glance

Fiscal year ended: October 1999

Revenue and net income in $ millions

	1995	1996	1997	1998	1999	4-Year Growth Average (%)	4-Year Growth Total (%)
Total Revenue	15,766	16,474	17,586	19,761	19,683	9.32	42.47
Net Income	1,262	1,430	1,679	1,824	1,757	11.83	56.03
Earnings/ Share ($)	3.49	4.09	4.91	5.3	5.01	13.65	66.14
Dividend/ Share ($)	1.18	1.33	1.52	1.76	1.88	11.13	51.72
Dividend Yield (%)	3.92	3	2.02	2.48	2.96	–	–
Price to Earnings (PE)	8.63	10.83	15.35	13.42	12.66	–	–

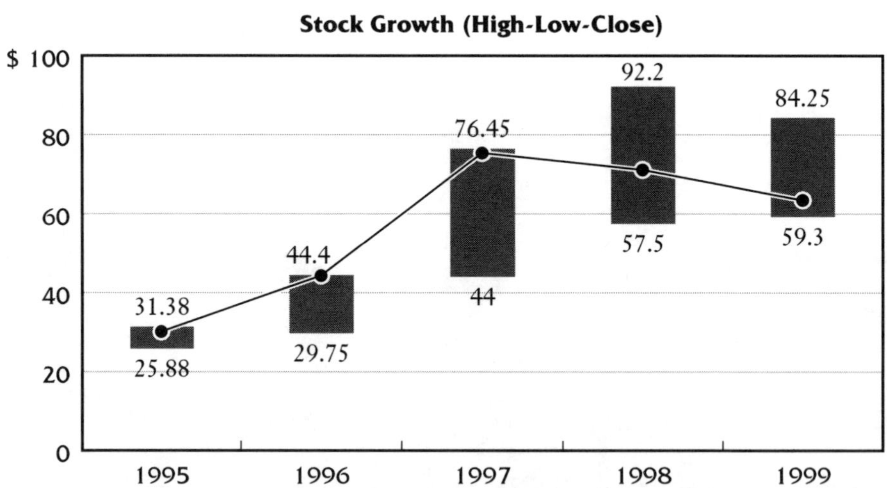

Close	30.13	44.3	75.35	71.1	63.45

45

E-L FINANCIAL CORPORATION LTD.

161 University Avenue, 10th Floor
Toronto, ON M5H 3B8
(416) 947-2578

President, Chairman: Hon. Henry N.R. Jackman

Revenue Growth	★
Pre-tax Income Growth	★★★
Total Return	★★★★★
Return on Capital Employed	–★
TSE: ELF	**8**

E-L Financial Corporation Ltd. is an investment holding company that owns 100 percent of The Dominion of Canada General Insurance Company and 80 percent of The Empire Life Insurance Company. The company also owns a portfolio of investments.

The company has been a steady, but not spectacular, performer. Its revenue and growth have been modest, but its five year total return of over 22 percent is impressive given the relatively low risk of E-L Financial's business. Like a number of the other financial services companies profiled in this book, the challenge and opportunity for E-L Financial will be in the steps it takes in the coming years, as the industry continues along the path of consolidation. Given the company's impressive and consistent double-digit return on capital over the past five years, E-L should stand out among its peer group as an attractive partner for other financial institutions.

The Dominion of Canada General Insurance Company underwrites property and casualty insurance across Canada, with operations focused on Ontario, Alberta, British Columbia, and the Maritimes. The Empire Life Insurance Company provides a range of life insurance products, as well as employee benefit plans and financial services, across Canada.

For fiscal 1998 (year ending December 31, 1998) the company reported revenue of $1.11 billion, versus $1.14 billion for fiscal 1997. Fiscal 1997 results include $110 million in realized gains from the company's sale of National Trustco Inc.

For fiscal 1998 insurance and annuity premiums accounted for approximately $841 million of revenue, with investment income (including sales of investments) accounting for $260 million. A further $26 million was derived from amortization.

For fiscal 1999, the company reported total revenue of $1.19 billion, of which $876 million came from insurance and annuity premiums, $258 million came from investment income (including sales of investments), and a further $53 million came from amortization.

E-L Financial Corporation is based in Toronto and employs approximately 630 people.

Revenue Growth: ★

Past five years: 7 percent

Pre-tax Income Growth: ★ ★ ★

Past five years: 13 percent

Total Return: ★ ★ ★ ★ ★

Past five years: 22 percent

Return on Capital Employed: –★

Past five years: –2 percent

E-L Financial Corporation Ltd. at a Glance

Fiscal year ended: Decmber 1999

Revenue and net income in $ millions

	1995	1996	1997	1998	1999	4-Year Growth Average (%)	4-Year Growth Total (%)
Total Revenue	900	965	1,135	1,109	1,186	7.09	30.35
Net Income	44	58	166	57	53	36.53	20.76
Earnings/ Share ($)	11.34	15.13	43.32	14.88	13.7	36.54	20.81
Dividend/ Share ($)	0.5	0.5	0.5	0.5	0.5	–	0
Dividend Yield (%)	0.56	0.39	0.22	0.23	0.36	–	–
Price to Earnings (PE)	7.94	8.46	5.27	14.45	10.22	–	–

Stock Growth (High-Low-Close)

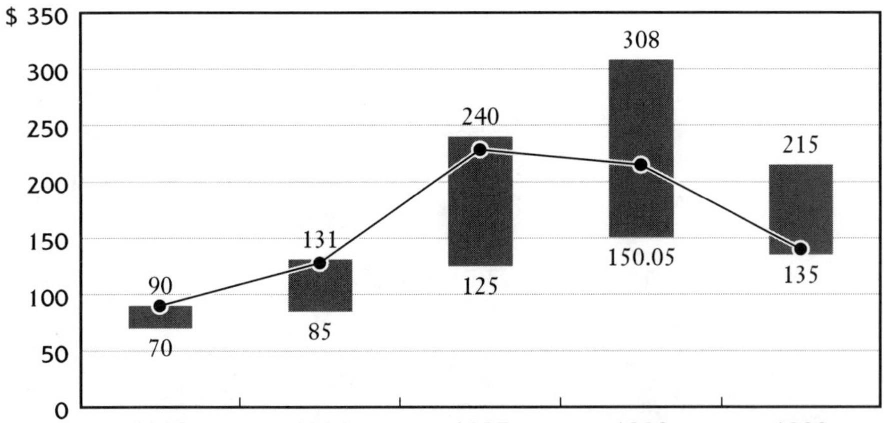

Close	90	128	228.5	215	140

46

WINPAK LTD.

100 Saulteaux Crescent
Winnipeg, MB R3J 3T3
(204) 889-1015

President, CEO: J.R. Lavery

Revenue Growth	★
Pre-tax Income Growth	★★★★
Total Return	★★★
Return on Capital Employed	0
TSE: WPK	**8**

Winpak Ltd. and its subsidiaries design, manufacture, and sell flexible and semi-flexible packaging materials. Its primary clients are North American perishable-food producers, although the company also manufactures and markets packaging products for industrial and medical purposes, as well as for filling machines.

The company's products include laminates (used for packaging food and beverage products, as well as pharmaceutical products), specialty films (used for packaging by the food, textile, medical, and furniture industries), modified atmosphere packaging (such as vacuum packaging), single-serving sanitary containers, and packaging equipment.

The company's packaging products are sold in North America, Mexico, the Caribbean, South America, and the United Kingdom, and its packaging machines are sold worldwide.

For fiscal 1999 (year ending December 31, 1999) the company reported revenue of $374 million, versus $336 million for fiscal 1998.

The company operates principally in Canada and the United States, with 11 production facilities in North America (including American Biaxis, see below). The company plans to close a plant in Pennsylvania during 2000, however, redistributing its production to other facilities.

In 1998 the company entered into a joint venture with the Nichimen Corporation of Tokyo, Japan, to produce a film necessary in the manufacture of some of Winpak's products. Nichimen will market production in excess of Winpak's needs. Winpak controls 51 percent of the new company, American Biaxis Inc., which has a manufacturing facility in Winnipeg that began operation in late 1999.

Winpak is headquartered in Winnipeg and employs approximately 1400 people.

The company's shares are listed on the Toronto and Winnipeg stock exchanges.

Revenue Growth: ★

Past five years: 7.4 percent

Pre-tax Income Growth: ★ ★ ★ ★

Past five years: 18 percent

Total Return: ★ ★ ★

Past five years: 14.9 percent

Return on Capital Employed: 0

Past five years: 4 percent

Winpak Ltd. at a Glance

Fiscal year ended: December 1999

Revenue and net income in $ millions

	1995	1996	1997	1998	1999	4-Year Growth Average (%)	4-Year Growth Total (%)
Total Revenue	281	292	300	336	374	7.47	33.02
Net Income	10	12	12	16	17	13.86	61.93
Earnings/ Share ($)	1.58	1.92	1.84	2.48	2.56	13.84	62.03
Dividend/ Share ($)	0.4	0.4	0.4	0.4	0.4	–	0
Dividend Yield (%)	1.63	1.2	1.01	0.83	0.7	–	–
Price to Earnings (PE)	15.51	17.32	21.47	19.35	22.27	–	–

Stock Growth (High-Low-Close)

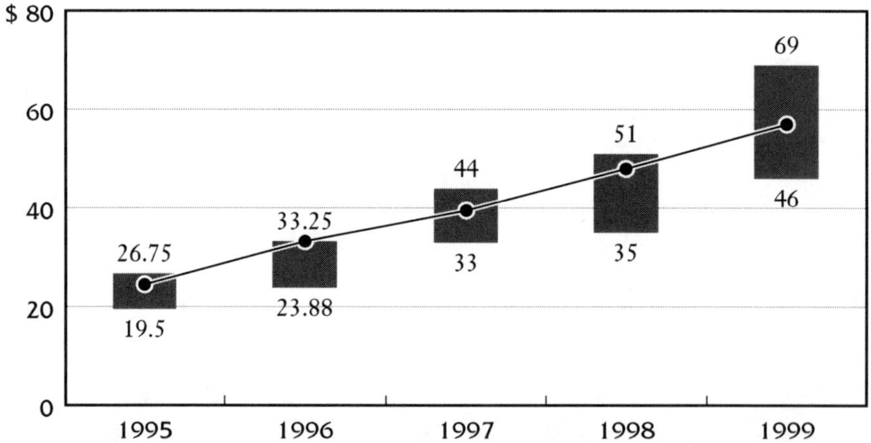

Close	24.5	33.25	39.5	48	57

47

ENBRIDGE INC.

421, 7th Avenue SW, Suite 2900
Calgary, AB T2P 4K9
(403) 231-3973
www.enbridge.com

President, CEO: B.F. MacNeil

Revenue Growth	0
Pre-tax Income Growth	★★★★
Total Return	★★★★★
Return on Capital Employed	–★
TSE: ENB	**8**

Enbridge Inc. is a Calgary-based oil, natural gas, and energy distribution and transportation company. The company is organized in five distinct business divisions: Liquids Pipelines, Gas Distribution, Gas Pipelines and New Business Development, International, and Energy Services.

Enbridge's Liquids Pipelines division operates the longest crude-oil and liquids pipeline system in the world: approximately 14,000 kilometres of pipeline in Canada and the United States, carrying over

2 million barrels of crude oil and other liquids per day. This system is built around the assets of Enbridge Pipelines Inc., a wholly owned subsidiary, as well as affiliated pipelines in Canada and Lakehead Pipe Line Partners (of which Enbridge owns roughly 15 percent) and other affiliates in the United States.

According to the company, the Liquids Pipelines division accounted for $600 million of total revenue of $2.7 billion in fiscal 1999 (year ending December 31, 1999). In fiscal 1998, these figures were $495 million and $2.3 billion, respectively.

In the Gas Distribution division, Enbridge Consumers Gas, Canada's largest natural gas distributor, serves approximately 1.5 million customers in Ontario, Quebec, and New York state. The company also distributes gas in New Brunswick through Enbridge Gas New Brunswick and, due to its 32 percent ownership in Noverco Inc., in Quebec and the northeastern United States. The Gas Distribution division reported revenue in fiscal 1999 of roughly $1.9 billion, versus $1.8 billion for the fiscal 1998.

The Gas Pipelines and New Business Development division is composed of the company's interest in a number of natural gas pipeline projects, as well as gas gathering, processing, and distribution services in western Canada. In fiscal 1999 this segment reported revenue of $55 million, versus $25 million in fiscal 1998.

Enbridge's International division consists of Enbridge International Inc. and Enbridge Technology Inc., which are responsible for managing Enbridge's interests in the OCENSA pipeline in Colombia. This segment also markets proprietary pipeline-operation technologies and training worldwide. Revenue for fiscal 1999 was reported to be $24 million, versus $16 million for fiscal 1998.

Finally, the Energy Services division supplies retail energy products and services, such as gas furnaces and air conditioning, in both Canada and the United States. In fiscal 1999 this accounted for revenue of approximately $143 million, versus $21 million in fiscal 1998.

The company explains that the large growth of this division is due to the transfer of some ancillary retailing business from the Gas Distribution division.

Like some of the other companies profiled in this book, Enbridge qualifies as a defensive investment by virtue of its relative immunity to economic cycles. After all, natural gas is not a luxury but a necessity. A generous dividend program also provides investors with an added safety net.

Enbridge employs approximately 5500 people in Canada, the United States, and South America.

The company is listed on the Toronto and Montreal stock exchanges, as well as on NASDAQ.

Revenue Growth: 0

Past five years: 4 percent

Pre-tax Income Growth: ★★★★

Past five years: 17 percent

Total Return: ★★★★★

Past five years: 22 percent

Return on Capital Employed: –★

Past five years: –5 percent

Enbridge Inc. at a Glance

Fiscal year ended: December 1999

Revenue and net income in $ millions

	1995	1996	1997	1998	1999	4-Year Growth Average (%)	4-Year Growth Total (%)
Total Revenue	2,323	2,458	2,520	2,342	2,688	4.01	15.71
Net Income	130	180	217	241	300	23.52	129.91
Earnings/ Share ($)	1.15	1.45	1.575	1.655	1.91	13.79	66.09
Dividend/ Share ($)	1	1.015	1.06	1.12	1.195	4.57	19.5
Dividend Yield (%)	6.27	5.08	3.24	3.18	4.17	–	–
Price to Earnings (PE)	13.86	13.78	20.76	21.3	15	–	–

Stock Growth (High-Low-Close)

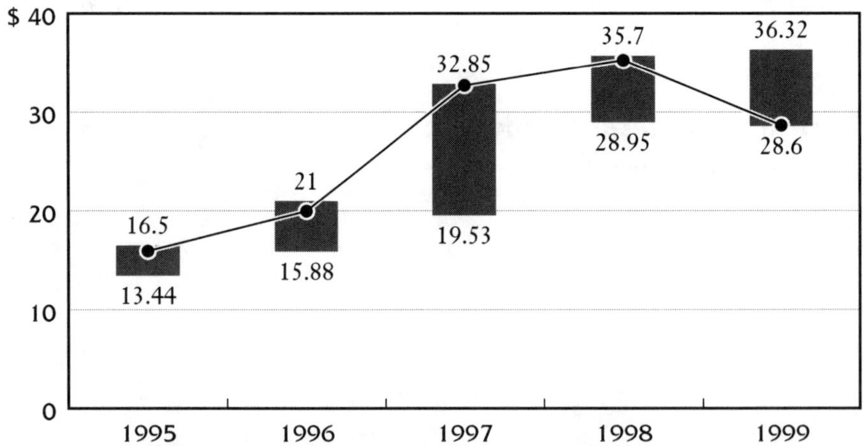

Close	15.94	19.98	32.7	35.25	28.65

48

DUPONT CANADA INC.

Box 2200, Streetsville
Mississauga, ON L5M 2H3
(905) 821-5358
www.dupont.ca

President, CEO: D.W. Colcleugh

Revenue Growth	0
Pre-tax Income Growth	★★
Total Return	★★★★★
Return on Capital Employed	0
TSE: DUP.A	**7**

As has been pointed out elsewhere in this book, much of the focus on "technology" has been limited to computers and telecommunications. This ignores the huge strides being made in materials science that will change everything from the type of garbage bags we use, to the golf balls we hit on Sunday afternoons, to the plastic in the dashboard of the cars we drive to work on Monday mornings. Companies like DuPont Canada are at the forefront of these "technologies." DuPont is an industrial chemical company whose products are divided into five business groups: Nylon Enterprise, Performance Coatings and Polymers, Specialty Fibres, Specialty Materials, and Specialty Polymers and Films.

The Nylon Enterprise group is responsible for producing nylon yarn, which is used in the manufacturing of a wide variety of products, from automotive and home carpeting to safety air bags, dental floss, clothing, and tires. This group also sells related chemicals that are used as food additives and in the manufacturing of pharmaceutical products. For fiscal 1999 (year ending December 31, 1999) the Nylon Enterprise segment accounted for $784 million of the company's total revenue of $2.2 billion (up from $2 billion in fiscal 1998).

The Performance Coatings and Polymers group sells automotive finishes and engineering polymers (nylon resins and plastics). DuPont supplies more new car and truck colours than any other paint manufacturer. This group accounted for revenue of $545 million in fiscal 1999.

The Specialty Fibres group accounted for $208 million in sales for fiscal 1999. This group produces fibres—including Lycra, Nomex, Kevlar, and Dacron—that are used in the manufacture of leisure and protective clothing.

The Specialty Materials group, which accounted for sales of $360 million in fiscal 1999, produces agricultural products such as herbicides, as well as fluorochemical refrigerants and propellants and white pigment and mineral products.

Finally, the Specialty Polymers and Films group is responsible for a wide variety of packaging materials (according to the company, 50 percent of all milk in Canada is packaged in pouches developed by DuPont Canada), as well as industrial adhesives and flooring and surface products. This group accounted for fiscal 1999 sales of $330 million.

Because so much media investor attention is focused on the new economy and on so-called technology stocks (Internet, computers, telecommunications), many investors have overlooked the considerable advances in materials technology that allow companies like Intel to make faster processors and wireless companies to build robust satellites. Again, DuPont represents a solid blue-chip investment that is just as much a part of the new world order as any dot-com company.

DuPont Canada is headquartered in Mississauga, Ontario, and employs approximately 3200 people.

As of March 4, 1999, 76 percent of the company was owned by Delaware-based E.I. du Pont de Nemours & Co.

DuPont Canada is listed on the Toronto and Montreal stock exchanges.

Revenue Growth: 0

Past five years: 4.9 percent

Pre-tax Income Growth: ★★

Past five years: 8 percent

Total Return: ★★★★★

Past five years: 22 percent

Return on Capital Employed: 0

Past five years: 3 percent

DuPont Canada Inc. at a Glance

Fiscal year ended: December 1999

Revenue and net income in $ millions

	1995	1996	1997	1998	1999	4-Year Growth Average (%)	4-Year Growth Total (%)
Total Revenue	1,862	1,853	1,924	2,049	2,245	4.85	20.58
Net Income	182	200	212	299	253	10.42	39.21
Earnings/ Share ($)	1.96	2.16	2.29	3.21	2.72	10.28	38.78
Dividend/ Share ($)	0.41	0.52	3.55	0.64	0.7	134.23	70.73
Dividend Yield (%)	1.71	1.63	10.13	1.49	1.18	–	–
Price to Earnings (PE)	12.24	14.79	15.31	13.4	21.82	–	–

Stock Growth (High-Low-Close)

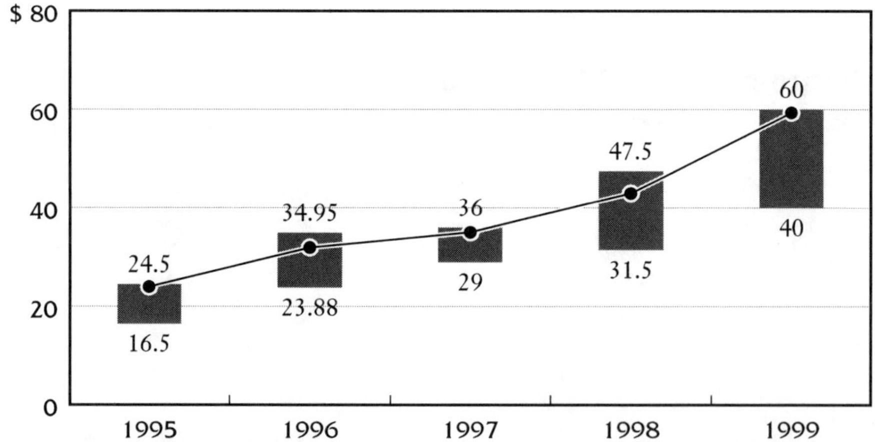

Close	24	31.95	35.05	43	59.35

49

SUNCOR ENERGY INC.

112, 4th Avenue SW, Box 38
Calgary, AB T2P 2V5
(403) 269-8670
www.suncor.com

President & CEO: R.L. George

Revenue Growth	★
Pre-tax Income Growth	★★
Total Return	★★★★★
Return on Capital Employed	–★
TSE: SU	**7**

Suncor Energy Inc. is involved in the exploration for and production and marketing of natural gas and crude oil. Through its Sunoco Inc. subsidiary, the company also refines crude oil and markets petroleum and petrochemical products.

Suncor's business is divided into three operating units:

- Sunoco, which markets petroleum products mainly in Ontario and petrochemical products in the United States and Europe.

Sunoco has its own subsidiary, Suncor Energy Marketing Inc., responsible for marketing products produced by Suncor's other two operating units.
- Oil Sands, which produces synthetic crude oils, diesel fuel, and other products from Alberta oil sands and markets them in both Canada and the United States.
- Exploration and Production, which explores for, develops, produces, and markets both crude oil (in Canada) and natural gas (in Canada and the United States).

In early 2000 Suncor created a new business development unit, In-Situ and International Oil, to oversee the company's Australian Stuart Oil Shale project and its in-situ (that is, heavy oil that can be extracted "in place" from oil sands) project in Alberta.

During 1999 Suncor's daily production was approximately 120,000 barrels of crude oil and natural-gas liquids (representing 6 percent of Canada's total crude-oil output) and 226 million cubic feet of natural gas.

For fiscal 1999 (year ending December 31, 1999) the company reported revenue of $2.4 billion, versus $2.1 billion in fiscal 1998.

As of December 31, 1999, the company reported proved gross crude-oil reserves of 35 million barrels and proved gross natural gas reserves of 1 trillion cubic feet. The company also reported proved and probable gross synthetic crude oil reserves of 2.5 billion barrels.

Headquartered in Calgary, Suncor Energy employs approximately 2800 people. Sunoco Inc. is headquartered in Toronto.

Revenue Growth: ★

Past five years: 6 percent

Pre-tax Income Growth: ★★

Past five years: 9 percent

Total Return: ★★★★★

Past five years: 30 percent

Return on Capital Employed: –★

Past five years: –12 percent

Suncor Energy Inc. at a Glance

Fiscal year ended: December 1999

Revenue and net income in $ millions

	1995	1996	1997	1998	1999	4-Year Growth Average (%)	4-Year Growth Total (%)
Total Revenue	1,901	2,100	2,154	2,070	2,387	6.11	25.57
Net Income	151	187	223	188	200	8.45	32.45
Earnings/ Share ($)	1.38	1.69	2.02	1.7	1.6	5.07	15.94
Dividend/ Share ($)	0.57	0.64	0.68	0.68	0.68	4.63	19.3
Dividend Yield (%)	2.67	2.25	1.39	1.48	1.13	–	–
Price to Earnings (PE)	15.47	16.8	24.26	27.06	37.75	–	–

Stock Growth (High-Low-Close)

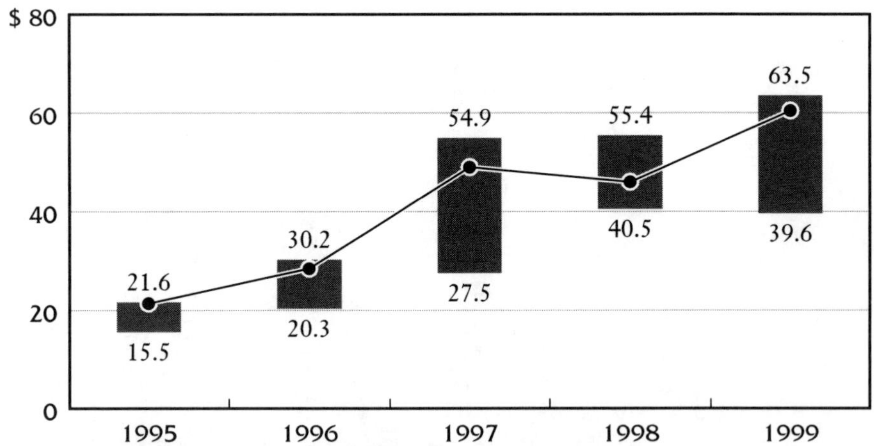

Close	21.35	28.4	49	46	60.4

50

POTASH CORPORATION OF SASKATCHEWAN INC.

500, 122 First Avenue South
Saskatoon, SK S7K 7G3
(306) 933-8500
www.potashcorp.com

Chairman & CEO: Charles E. Childers
President & COO: William J. Doyle

Revenue Growth	★★★★★
Pre-tax Income Growth	–★
Total Return	★
Return on Capital Employed	–★
TSE: POT	**4**

Potash Corporation of Saskatchewan Inc. (PCS) is the largest fertilizer enterprise in the world, mining and producing the three primary plant nutrients: potash, nitrogen, and phosphate. The company sells worldwide to three key sectors: agriculture, where, as noted, the company is the largest producer of fertilizers in the world; animal nutrition, where the company is the world's largest producer of phosphate feed ingredients; and industrial chemicals, where the company is the largest producer of industrial nitrogen products.

The company mines potash mainly in Canada (it has one mining operation in the United States) and has approximately one-quarter of the world's potash capacity. According to the company, it has over a century of potash reserves. PCS produces two dozen grades of potash fertilizer. Potash also has industrial uses (including television/computer screens, soaps, perfumes, and water softeners) and is a feed supplement for livestock and poultry.

Nitrogen products (starting with ammonia) are manufactured by PCS in the United States and Trinidad. In addition to feedstock and fertilizer applications, nitrogen products have a wide variety of industrial uses, including construction, pharmaceuticals, batteries, tires, paints, and plastics.

Phosphate is both mined (as phosphate ore) and manufactured (as phosphoric acid) in the United States. It, too, is mainly used in fertilizers and feed for livestock, but it also has industrial applications, such as in the manufacture of soft drinks and detergents.

Revenue for fiscal 1999 (year ending December 31, 1999) was $2.9 billion, versus $3.5 billion for fiscal 1998. Of fiscal 1999 revenue, phosphate business accounted for $754 million, nitrogen business for $744 million, and potash business for $563 million.

PCS is headquartered in Saskatoon and employs approximately 5700 people.

Shares of PCS trade on the Toronto, Montreal, and New York stock exchanges.

Revenue Growth: ★★★★★

Past five years: 32 percent

Pre-tax Income Growth: –★

Past five years: –25 percent

Total Return: ★

Past five years: 7 percent

Return on Capital Employed: –★

Past five years: –42 percent

Potash Corporation of Saskatchewan Inc. at a Glance

Fiscal year ended: December 1999

Revenue and net income in US$ millions

	1995	1996	1997	1998	1999	4-Year Growth Average (%)	4-Year Growth Total (%)
Total Revenue	1,168	1,924	3,327	3,532	2,995	32.15	156.42
Net Income	218	287	426	399	–599	–43.97	–375.14
Earnings/ Share ($)	5.021	6.291	8.125	7.377	–11.045	–51.12	–319.98
Dividend/ Share ($)	1.446	1.453	1.473	1.469	1.469	–0.11	–0.48
Dividend Yield (%)	1.49	1.25	1.24	1.49	2.09	–	–
Price to Earnings (PE)	19.27	18.55	14.65	13.35	N/A	–	–

Stock Growth (High-Low-Close)

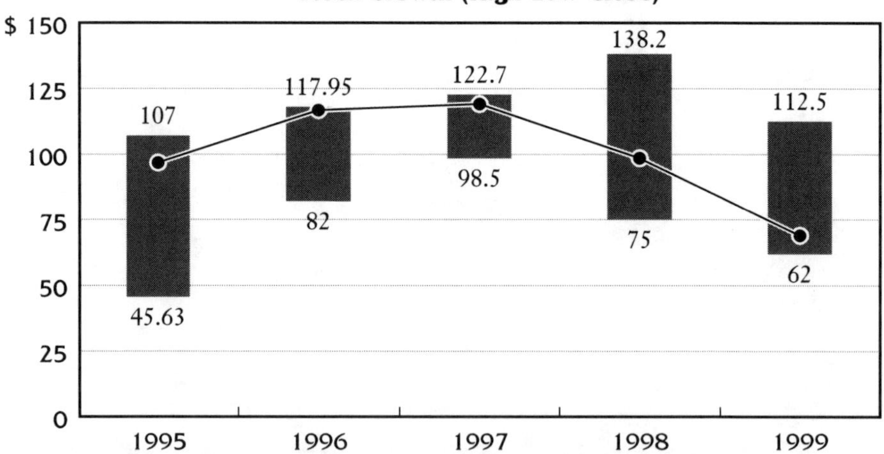

Close	96.75	116.7	119.05	98.5	69

THE 50 BEST STOCKS IN ALPHABETICAL ORDER

AGF Management Ltd. (16)
ATI Technologies Inc. (2)
ATS Automation
Tooling Systems Inc. (20)
BCE Inc. (36)
Bombardier Inc. (34)
Brascan Corp. (42)
Canadian National Railway Co. (17)
Canadian Pacific Ltd. (22)
CGI Group Inc. (4)
C-Mac Industries Inc. (24)
Creo Products Inc. (3)
Cogeco Inc. (10)
Cognos Inc. (6)
Corby Distilleries Ltd. (13)
Dorel Industries Inc. (1)
DuPont Canada Inc. (48)
E-L Financial Corporation Ltd. (45)
Empire Company Ltd. (25)
Enbridge Inc. (47)
Ensign Resource
Service Group Inc. (28)
Four Seasons Hotels Inc. (5)
Imperial Oil Ltd. (39)
Intertape Polymer Group Inc. (40)
Intrawest Corp. (8)
Jean Coutu Group (PJC) (31)
Leitch Technology Corp. (32)
Leon's Furniture Ltd. (35)
Linamar Corp. (30)
Loblaw Companies Ltd. (27)
Magna International Inc. (21)
Maple Leaf Foods Inc. (37)
McGraw-Hill Ryerson Ltd. (7)
MDS Inc. (33)
Moffat Communications Ltd. (29)
Nova Chemicals Corp. (14)
Onex Corp. (11)
Penn West Petroleum Ltd. (19)
Potash Corp. of Saskatchewan Inc. (50)
Rio Alto Exploration Ltd. (12)
Royal Bank of Canada (44)
Royal Group Technologies Ltd. (38)
Sears Canada Inc. (18)
Shaw Communications Inc. (15)
Suncor Energy Inc. (49)
Thomson Corp. (23)
Toronto Dominion Bank (9)
Unican Security Systems Ltd. (41)
A. L. Van Houtte Ltée (26)
Wescast Industries Inc. (43)
Winpak Ltd. (46)

INDEX

Look for these other titles in the 50 BEST for CANADIANS series

The 50 Best Internet Stocks for Canadians: Long Term Investing in the Internet Economy
Mark Pavan, Gene Walden, and Tom Shaughnessy
ISBN 0-7715-7721-4

Don't get burned with an unlucky guess… use this book to learn more about investing in Internet stocks, and see which companies have outperformed their peers.

The 50 Best Stocks for Under $20 for Canadians
Philip Benson and Gene Walden
ISBN 0-7715-7706-0

The ultimate guide to Canadian small-cap stocks! They won't be under $20 for long…

The 50 Best Ethical Stocks for Canadians: High Value Investing
Deb Abbey and Michael C. Jantzi
ISBN 0-7715-7695-1

Two of Canada's leading authorities on social investing team up to show you how to invest with your values without compromising on returns.